Yuri Shulipa

Judicial monitoring to protect the rights of car owners

Yuri Shulipa

Judicial monitoring to protect the rights of car owners

ScienciaScripts

Imprint

Any brand names and product names mentioned in this book are subject to trademark, brand or patent protection and are trademarks or registered trademarks of their respective holders. The use of brand names, product names, common names, trade names, product descriptions etc. even without a particular marking in this work is in no way to be construed to mean that such names may be regarded as unrestricted in respect of trademark and brand protection legislation and could thus be used by anyone.

Cover image: www.ingimage.com

This book is a translation from the original published under ISBN 978-3-659-54887-1.

Publisher:
Sciencia Scripts
is a trademark of
Dodo Books Indian Ocean Ltd. and OmniScriptum S.R.L publishing group

120 High Road, East Finchley, London, N2 9ED, United Kingdom
Str. Armeneasca 28/1, office 1, Chisinau MD-2012, Republic of Moldova, Europe
Printed at: see last page
ISBN: 978-620-7-76416-7

Copyright © Yuri Shulipa
Copyright © 2024 Dodo Books Indian Ocean Ltd. and OmniScriptum S.R.L publishing group

TABLE OF CONTENTS:

Yu Yu Shulipa
Judicial monitoring to protect the rights of car owners
Author - Head of Legal Department of the Federation of Russian Motor Owners

The present work is devoted to legal, organisational and tactical aspects of public control over the activities of the traffic <u>police</u> and courts of general jurisdiction and, together with them, the protection of the rights of the individual car owner.

It is intended for representatives of public associations exercising public control over law enforcement activities, practicing lawyers, researchers in the field of administrative and constitutional law, criminology, sociologists, political scientists, specialists in the field of road safety, civil and social activists, drivers of vehicles, as well as for all those interested in protecting the rights of car owners.

Three things that create obstacles to normal traffic: irresponsibility of competent officials, road patrol service, roads of Russia.

Y. SCHULIPA

Introduction

In modern Russia, car owners are one of the most unprotected social groups from the arbitrary behaviour of the authorities. Citizens are tired of constant lawlessness of traffic police inspectors and judges of courts of general jurisdiction. This situation is caused by the imperfection of the current legislation and the vicious practice of its application.

The federal policy of the authorities in the field of road traffic safety is reduced only to the regular toughening of administrative penalties and at the same time to the reduction of the scope of rights of persons brought to administrative responsibility.

Carrying out administrative-jurisdictional activity of traffic police inspectors and judges of courts of general jurisdiction are not engaged in the elimination of causes and conditions contributing to the commission of administrative offences, but are limited to a formal-punitive approach. This means that the inspector and the judge are interested only in formal fulfilment of the requirements of the procedures established by law, on initiation and further movement of the case.

Traffic police inspectors cannot reduce the number of prosecutions or protocols compared to the same period last year if they want to receive a positive evaluation of their performance. It is also favourable for career development and increase of allowances for judges to handle as many cases as possible. In fact, mostly judges play the role of prosecutors, try to find any, more often invented clue, in order not to take into account the evidence of innocence presented by car owners, do not make mental and physical efforts when considering cases, rewrite accusatory stories from the protocols and on their basis make accusatory rulings.

In this regard, the first chapter of the manual is devoted to a detailed analysis of the organisational and legal aspect of the prosecutorial-punitive collusion of the traffic police and courts, without which the emergence of judicial monitoring would be impossible. In this chapter, along with traditional methods, new more effective ways of protecting the rights of car owners are considered.

The paper is conditioned by the conclusion that at the current stage of state and legal development of Russia it is impossible to eliminate corrupt practices and various abuses on the part of traffic police inspectors and judges of courts of general jurisdiction on the initiative of competent officials of public authorities. This means that in the near future the situation in the sphere of legality of justice and executive power will inevitably worsen. The top leadership of the country is unwilling and unable to offer even minimal positive changes in this sphere. Therefore, the change of the situation depends only on the degree of activity and organisation of citizens themselves. The situation can be improved "from below" with the help of professional monitoring, which is confirmed by practice. A properly organised and stable judicial monitoring system can, if not completely eliminate various corrupt practices and abuses in individual courts, at least minimise their manifestation.

A judge's actions during the consideration of a case and judicial acts are the subject of judicial monitoring. Thanks to the processing of information contained in the rulings of justices of the peace posted on the Internet portals of the courts, it has become possible to promptly identify corruption crossroads and take public response measures based on the results of the identification.

The results of judicial monitoring, when studying the rulings issued by the same judge in cases initiated at the same intersection, allow to identify the bias of the judge in the outcome of the case. For example, when under the same circumstances, after the flow of rulings on deprivation of driving licence, there are rulings on imposition of administrative fines, or on terminated cases.

After all, one of the main tasks of judicial monitoring is to compel officials and judges to carry out their professional activities within the framework of the law.

Due to shortcomings in the legislation on administrative offences, traffic police inspectors and judges work in almost a single organisational and legal relationship, which enables judicial monitoring to collect the necessary data not only on the activities of the courts, but also on the activities of the executive authorities.

The novelty of the work consists in a step-by-step description of the algorithm of implementation of public control over the activities of traffic police inspectors and judges of courts of general jurisdiction; detailed consideration of the main falsifications of evidence in cases of administrative offences, including those obtained through improper use of measuring devices. Practically all legal, organisational, technical and tactical aspects of public control are considered. A separate section is devoted to the participation of a specialist in the case.

The materials of this paper are also intended to help car owners avoid all suits of abuses by traffic police inspectors and judges.

The paper defines such simultaneously new and important concepts as **"Judicial Monitor"**, **"Citizen Patrol"**, **"Corruption Crossroads"**, **"Public Representative"** *and* so on.

At the end of many sentences there are references to the relevant normative legal acts, which makes it possible, when using the manual, to timely and materially confirm to the opponents the rightness of their actions, and to refute their illegal actions.

Thus, the manual is intended for hourly use in practice.

CHAPTER 1

ORGANISATIONAL AND LEGAL ASPECT OF ACCUSATORY-PUNITIVE COLLUSION BETWEEN THE G.I.B.D.D. AND THE COURTS

1.1 12 Reasons for collusion between traffic police and courts

Due to the imperfection of the current legislation and inadequate organisational support, traffic police inspectors and justices of the peace are forced to interact in a single organisational and legal relationship. The phenomenon arising on the basis of this interaction, when the judge initially unreasonably does not trust the testimony of the car owner, and - accusatory materials and explanations of the traffic police inspector is called collusion.

The collusion between the traffic police and the courts has led to a violation of the rule of law, caused massive violations of the rights and legitimate interests of citizens, and is a threat to the legal and strategic security of our state. The collusion causes material and moral damage to individuals and legal entities.

The collusion of traffic police and courts often leads to violations of the rights of subjects of economic activity by destabilising road transport. Due to police and judicial arbitrariness, having lost their driving licence, many citizens have simultaneously lost their only source of income and social stability and have been pushed to the brink of survival.

As a consequence, many people suffering from various forms of mental disorders and diseases have appeared in society. The problems of alcoholism and drug addiction have become more acute, and the mortality rate among the able-bodied population of the country has increased.

The colossal number of unjust judicial acts has significantly increased the corruption component in the field of road safety. It is often impossible for car owners to prove the legality of their actions in courts, which inevitably led to an increase in the amount of bribes to roadside traffic police inspectors. In fact, the consideration of cases on administrative offences has turned into a mass deception of citizens.

The unlawful collusion of traffic police and courts has long ago outgrown the legal framework in the form of intent and has given rise to offences against state power and law enforcement service, resulting in significant violations of citizens' rights.[1] When considering each specific case by the court, judicial norm control is obliged to ensure legality in the activities of traffic police inspectors.

The lack of proper judicial norm control, the implementation of formal prosecutor's supervision and control over the activities of traffic police inspectors by the DSS and higher management led to the failure to solve the majority of crimes related to theft of vehicles, robbery of heavy vehicles, causing death or serious harm to the health of road users, and contributed to the commission of terrorist acts.

In other words, the problem of unlawful collusion of traffic police *and* courts is the most dangerous, serious, threatening to each of us and the country as a whole.

The empirical basis of the study was formed by the materials of the electrotransport.ru website, analysis of law enforcement practice of the courts of Moscow and 12 subjects of the Russian Federation in the field of road safety, relevant normative legal acts, materials of the FAR Commission on counteracting unlawful collusion between traffic police and courts, interviews with former and current judges, traffic police inspectors, prosecutors and special services, interviews with persons brought to administrative responsibility, observations of the activities of individual representatives of traffic police and judges, the author's participation as a defence counsel in cases of administrative

---

[1] Shulipa Y. Y. Moscow judge legalised official offences. M-2010. Moscow branch of FAR: www. far-msk.ru/?p=9615

offences, and the author's participation in the investigation of administrative offences.

1) . Collusion starts on the road.

The rights of a car owner to a fair and impartial court are violated as soon as a report is drawn up. Practice shows that in 99 out of 100 cases, immediately after drawing up a report, traffic police inspectors notify car owners about the consideration of cases against them in court. And not only in cases involving an exceptional punishment in the form of deprivation of the right to drive a vehicle, but also in cases that allow as an alternative punishment of an administrative fine or arrest.

The legality of such a notification raises serious doubts. How did the judge suddenly know that exactly on a particular day and hour the car owner should commit an administrative offence? In addition, none of the current acts does not impose on the traffic police inspector the obligation to notify the person brought to administrative responsibility, about the place and time of consideration of the case in court.

By virtue of para. 2 part. 1 part 1 of article 29.4. of the CAO RF the obligation to notify the participants of administrative proceedings is imposed exclusively on the judge or official, in whose proceedings the initiated case was received.

Before taking the case to judicial proceedings, according to para. 4 part 1 of Art. 29.4. 1 part 1 of article 29.4 of the CAO RF, the judge must establish the correctness of the protocol and other materials of the case. If the protocol is drawn up by an ineligible official and (or) improperly executed, as well as other case materials, the judge shall be obliged to make a determination to return the protocol on an administrative offence and other case materials to the body, official who initiated the case.

The traffic police inspector also has no right to notify directly from the road about the place and time of consideration of a case at the traffic police department by an inspector of administrative practice. The above norm also applies to the official authorised to consider cases on administrative offences.

A judge (official) who allows officials interested in the outcome of a case to interfere in his procedural activities is unlikely to issue a ruling based on the law.

Notification of the car owner knowingly presumes his guilt in committing an administrative offence and indicates the presence of bias and accusatory bias of the judge (official), to the person in respect of whom the case was initiated.

2) . Gaps in legislation and impunity.

In our opinion, the causes and conditions for the formation of unlawful collusion consist of three aspects: legal, tactical and organisational. Moreover, the legal aspect is a derivative of the tactical and organisational aspects.

Initially, the reasons for the formation of unlawful collusion of representatives of traffic police, justices of the peace and federal judges of courts of general jurisdiction lie in the current legislation. Let us turn to the norms of the CAO RF, practice and statistics of their application.

The majority of cases on administrative offences initiated by traffic police inspectors are considered by magistrates. As is known, these are part 4 of Art. 12.15, **"Driving in violation of the Rules of Road Traffic on the lane intended for oncoming traffic"**, part 4 of Art. 12.9, "Exceeding the established speed limit" (considered by both the traffic police authority and the justice of the peace. 4 of Art. 12.9, **"Exceeding the established speed limit"** (considered by both the traffic police and a justice of the peace), Art. 12.8, **"Driving a vehicle by an intoxicated driver, transfer of control of a vehicle to an intoxicated person",** and so on.

By virtue of the provisions of Art. 28.1. - 28.3. of the CAO an inspector of traffic police initiates a case on an administrative offence, entailing deprivation of the right to drive a vehicle, and the judge, in accordance with Art. 23.1. of the CAO RF, considers it.

Practice shows that complaints against the actions of traffic police inspectors in drawing up protocols drawn up under articles of the Code of Administrative Offences providing for deprivation of the right to drive a vehicle are considered in only a few cases.

Responses of the heads of traffic police departments to citizens' complaints are usually as follows. *Your complaint has been considered. Since in accordance with part 1 of article 23.1 of the CAO the case under part 4 of article 12.15 of the CAO RF is considered by a magistrate, the management of the traffic police department has no right to consider it.*

Notwithstanding the above legal provisions, the heads of traffic police departments are not entitled to avoid the obligation to take disciplinary measures for unlawful drawing up of protocols against their subordinates, since a citizen lodges a complaint about the unlawful actions of traffic police inspectors in drawing up a protocol and does not require the management of the traffic <u>police</u> department to consider the case brought against him.

By virtue of a number of departmental orders of the Ministry of Internal Affairs of the Russian Federation, the management of the traffic police department is obliged to monitor the activities of traffic police inspectors and, if necessary, apply for disciplinary measures against them.

The situation is somewhat similar when citizens file complaints with the prosecutor's office.

Citizens' complaints are often left without consideration and, in violation of part 5 of article 10 of the Federal Law "On the Prosecutor's Office of the Russian Federation", are forwarded to the management of traffic police departments, where, based on the results of the consideration of complaints, citizens receive similar replies.

Based on the provisions of Articles 52 and 53 of the Federal Law "On Police", the prosecutor's office supervises the activities of the police. Therefore, in such cases, prosecutors, as well as heads of traffic police departments, have no right to refrain from checking the actions of traffic police inspectors on the legality and validity of drawing up protocols.

The situation is somewhat different in cases involving administrative penalties in the form of a fine or deprivation of the right to drive a vehicle.

Cases on administrative offences entailing deprivation of the right to drive a vehicle or an administrative fine are considered both by officials of the traffic police and by magistrates or federal judges.

A significant proportion of such cases are considered by judges when the officials to whom cases of such administrative offences are brought refer them for consideration by judges.

The official of the traffic police authority shall refer the case to the court for consideration if he/she considers that the punishment imposed by him/her will be clearly insufficient. Let us consider the operation of this mechanism in a practical context.

The practice of consideration of these cases shows the following. If the motorist in the group of analysis does not agree with the imputed administrative offence, disputes its events or composition, points to the wrong qualification of the act, provides evidence refuting guilt in the imputed offence, the inspector of administrative practice sends the case to court, so that the judge imposed a penalty in the form of deprivation of the right to drive a vehicle.

Subsequently, despite the above circumstances, in 99 out of 100 cases magistrates issue conviction rulings on deprivation of the right to drive and rarely limit themselves to imposing punishment in the form of an administrative fine.

Meanwhile, the requirements of Articles 24.1, 26.1 of the CAO RF oblige traffic police officials, as well as judges, to consider cases on administrative offences, to resolve them in accordance with the law, while exercising normative control over the actions of traffic police inspectors to draw up protocols. Since the actions of a traffic police inspector (including departmental regulations and other norms) are the basis for drawing up a protocol and initiation of a case on an administrative offence.

In most cases, traffic <u>police</u> officials completely ignore the requirements of these norms.

In other words: if you agree with the offence imputed by the traffic <u>police,</u> even if you did not actually commit it, you will pay a fine; if you do not agree, you will be deprived of your licence for a certain period of time. And in this case, the court is used by the officials of the traffic police as an object of imposing the harshest possible punishment. It is no other way than to make the motorist more agreeable to the roadside traffic police inspector after several months of "fitness" on foot.[2]

Appealing with a complaint to the management of the traffic <u>police</u> department, whose inspector made the report (issued the resolution), means an unnecessary loss of time and is in itself ineffective. The traffic police system has its own customs. In order to imitate the service activity, the higher management is interested in more protocols drawn up and rulings issued.[3]

If, for example, a battalion commander punishes his subordinate employee, it is considered that there is a part of his fault, shortcomings in the performance of his direct duties. In order not to spoil the performance indicators, the management of the traffic police department, whose inspector has violated the law, is limited at best to a formal conversation with him, but in reality he remains unpunished, and, as we know, impunity breeds lawlessness. In addition, the decision taken by the traffic police inspector against the driver remains in force.[4]

Согласно приказу МВД РФ № 25 от 19.01.2010 г. "The rule according to which IAB units cannot reduce the number of prosecuted persons as compared to the same period of the previous year, if they want to receive a positive assessment of their performance, remains in place.

3) . Unlawful law enforcement.

The ideal condition for the formation of collusion between traffic police and courts is an entrenched enforcement practice that is not based on the law.

Law enforcement practice shows that the Presidium of the Supreme Court of the Russian Federation does not exercise proper supervision over the legality of judicial acts, in particular, in cases on administrative offences issued by courts of general jurisdiction.

Therefore, the final formation of law enforcement practice is closed on the presidiums of regional courts. Currently, it is the presidiums of regional courts that form law enforcement practice for regional judges specialising in consideration of cases on administrative offences. This circumstance is taken advantage of by unscrupulous judges.

One example is the unlawful refusal to satisfy the request to consider the case at the place of residence. Let us consider it on the example of judicial law enforcement practice in Moscow. Moscow.

Many justices of the peace often half-jokingly told us that there were some instructions from the Presidium of the Moscow City Court that prohibited referring cases to the place of residence within the city.[5]

By giving an unlawful refusal to satisfy the request to consider cases at the place of residence,

---

[2] Shulipa Yu. Yu. How can a driver appeal against a resolution on an administrative offence? M-2008. Electrotransport.ru: electrotransport.ru/ussr/index.php/topic,397.0.html

[3] Ibid.

[4] Ibid.

[5] Shulipa Yu. Yu. Diagnostics of Moscow administrative justice. First results on the example of corruption crossroads - Paveletskaya Square of Moscow. Moscow. Scientific and practical report. M-2011. Moscow branch of FAR: www.far-msk.ru/?page_id=H241

the leadership of the Presidium of Moscow City Court apparently has an interest in ensuring that cases on administrative offences are considered exclusively at the place of their initiation, i.e. in "forced places". Practice shows that many traffic police inspectors, due to regular visits to the same court stations as witnesses and for the transfer of cases, are on friendly terms with justices of the peace. Initially, it is the justices of the peace who shape law enforcement practice.

Such **"interaction"** often causes irreparable harm to persons brought to administrative responsibility, which, due to the existing accusatory-punitive law enforcement practice, in higher courts can no longer be corrected.[6]

This fact is confirmed by supervisory decisions of the Deputy Chairman of the Moscow City Court A. N. Dmitriev in which, from the standpoint of the law and the Constitutional Court of the Russian Federation, as well as the guiding explanations of the Supreme Court of the Russian Federation, the unlawful refusal to satisfy applications for consideration of cases at the place of residence was repeatedly recognised as "lawful".[7]

Therefore, based on the decisions of district courts and supervisory rulings, justices of the peace unlawfully refuse to grant applications for consideration of cases at the place of residence of citizens. Practice shows that judges bear absolutely no responsibility for these actions.

4) . NONDDL and SPT in the absence of independent judges.

The courts of the country have a unique practice in the world of justice in considering cases on administrative offences. Even if 20 witnesses testify in favour of the car owner, and the car owner himself provides the court with evidence justifying his actions, in 99 out of 100 cases the judge will believe the traffic police inspector who testified against the car owner and, on the basis of his testimony and accusatory materials drawn up by him on his own (often unsubstantiated) conviction, will issue a guilty verdict. The testimony of 20 witnesses from among citizens and the evidence presented by the car owner will be evaluated critically by the judge. Law enforcement practice shows that magistrate and federal judges deliberately invent motives for "critically" evaluating evidence in favour of car owners.

The presence of NONDDL (no grounds to distrust an official) and PPP (presumption of the police officer's rightness) in law enforcement practice, as well as the absence of independent judges significantly increased the level of corruption among traffic police inspectors and resulted in the violation of the legitimate interests of car owners.

5) . Violations of the rule of law.

It follows from the practice of consideration of cases that traffic police inspectors, justices of the peace and federal judges do not fulfil the main tasks of the CAO, aimed at the protection of the individual, the protection of human and civil rights and freedoms, the established procedure for the exercise of state power, public safety and prevention of administrative offences (article 1.2. of the CAO RF).

The presumption of innocence is violated (Art. 1.5. of the CAO RF).

In violation of the provisions of part 1 of article 1.6. CAO RF, persons brought to administrative responsibility are subjected to administrative penalties and measures to ensure proceedings on a case on an administrative offence without the grounds and outside the procedure established by law.

The tasks of administrative proceedings aimed at full, objective and timely clarification of the circumstances of each case, its resolution in accordance with the law, identification of causes and

---

[6] Ibid.

[7] Decision of the Deputy Chairman of the Moscow City Court of 17. 12. 2010, № 4a-3528/10

conditions that contributed to the commission of administrative offences are regularly violated (article 24.1. of the CAO RF).

In violation of part 1 of article 29.13. of the CAO RF, when establishing the causes of administrative offences and the conditions that contributed to their commission, no submissions are made to the relevant organisations and relevant officials on taking measures to eliminate these causes and conditions.

6) . Inappropriate organisational aspect.

As noted above, the organisational aspect of collusion between the traffic police and the courts is formed from the legal aspect.

The symbiosis between justices of the peace (federal) and traffic police officers, due to regular interaction, in connection with the transfer of cases and summoning the latter as witnesses, is a favourable moment for the judge to vent his anger on the driver, and the judge, accordingly, to meet his automotive needs. Through a traffic police inspector a judge can solve a number of car problems, both personal and those of his relatives, relatives, friends and acquaintances: to put (deregister) a car from the registry, to draw up a favourable and quick traffic accident, to find ways to neighbouring traffic police departments to exempt the above-mentioned persons from administrative and often criminal punishment, and even to buy confiscated cars through grey schemes. It is important for a traffic police inspector to make a guilty verdict out of the indictment report drawn up by him.

Practice shows that many traffic police inspectors, due to regular visits to the same court stations as witnesses, are on friendly terms with justices of the peace.

For example, in some judicial precincts, before cases were heard, DSS inspectors were in the offices of justices of the peace and federal judges and discussed solutions to personal problems.

7) . Collaborative Tactics.

In addition to judicial law enforcement practice and regular visits of traffic police inspectors to court hearings, sources of unlawful collusion include quarterly joint meetings of justices of the peace and federal judges with representatives of the traffic police.

The Commission on counteraction to unlawful collusion of traffic police and courts studied the minutes of scheduled meetings of justices of the peace and federal judges with traffic police inspectors. As a result, the Commission came to the unanimous opinion that the traffic police and the court have become a single punitive body of conveyor type. The phrases of some protocols indicate the existence of telephone rather than procedural relations between judges and traffic police inspectors, and traffic police inspectors use judicial power to make the decisions they want. In turn, some judges are also interested in punishing car owners. All this is a direct source of bias, corruption, lawlessness and leads to massive violation of citizens' rights.[8]

8) . Pressure on judges.

Besides, such relations between law enforcement bodies take place through exchange of letters containing explanations on certain issues.[9] For example, by an information letter of 27.12.2005, the Chairman of the Arkhangelsk Regional Court M.G. Averin demanded from the chairmen of district (city) courts and justices of the peace to change the law enforcement practice on a number of categories of cases.[10]

---

[8] Commission reveals joint traffic police and judicial methods of deceiving citizens. M - 2011. Moscow branch of FAR: www.far-msk.ru/?p=12164

[9] Shulipa Y. Y. Comments on law enforcement practice. M- 2008. Era-auto: www.car- era.ru/articles/2685.html

[10] Information letter of the Arkhangelsk Regional Court of 27.12.2005 on the issue of consideration of cases on administrative offences in the field of road traffic.

District (city) and regional courts also hold training and methodological meetings at which the work of judges is analysed on a quarterly basis and the results of their work in administering justice and organising case management are summarised. Often at such meetings, judges who issue acquittal orders and decisions are subjected to unlawful and unjustified criticism by the leadership of the courts concerned.

9) . Fear of the traffic police.

Often judges are afraid of spoiling established relationships with traffic police inspectors.

By issuing acquittal rulings and decisions, judges fear possible complaints from traffic police representatives to the presidents of district (city) and regional courts, as well as to the bodies of the judicial community.

By stipulating in Part 1.1, Article 30.1 and Part 5, Article 30.9. The lawmaker has equated them to the participants of the proceedings on the case by providing for the right of traffic police inspectors, who have drawn up the report and issued a decision, to appeal against court rulings and decisions.

In addition, the leadership of the traffic police department has the right to appeal to the prosecutor to protest against judicial acts that have entered into force or have not entered into force. Each cancelled ruling or decision in a district (regional) court inevitably worsens the performance of the judge.12

10) . A common interest in deceiving the population.

In general, representatives of the traffic police and judges are united by common interests to deceive the population.

Judges work for statistics. Judges benefit from hearing as many cases as possible.[11] Judges try to find any, more often invented clue in order not to take into account the evidence of innocence presented by drivers, they do not make mental and physical efforts when considering cases, they try to rewrite from the protocol the story of the accusation and on its basis to make a guilty verdict.[12]

The career of a judge depends, in particular, on the volume of cases. As practice shows, judges who massively issued conviction rulings on deprivation of driving licence, as it is called "by copying", quite quickly moved from justices of the peace to the category of federal judges and were even appointed as presidents of district courts.

As discussed above, traffic police inspectors also have an interest in drawing up more administrative protocols.

At joint planning meetings, plans are developed for the drafting of protocols by traffic police inspectors and the issuance of indictments by magistrates.

11). Intradepartmental corporate interest. In sum, these circumstances are generated by intra-departmental corporate reasons of the MIA. Both of the following reasons are at the root of the formation of collusion between the GIBDD and the courts.

The motives of the traffic police to increase the statistics on detected offences and crimes are as follows.

If there are so many traffic offences in the country, then we are needed. It means we need new equipment, premises, positions, etc., privileges. In other words, by increasing the statistics of offences, the traffic police justifies its existence.

---

[11] Arbitrariness of traffic police and courts. Materials of the press conference on 1 December 2010. Moscow branch of FAR: www.far-msk.ru/?p=10594

[12] Ibid.

12) . Failure to self-cleanse.

The renaming of **"militia"** to **"police"** did not bring about any positive changes in the activities of the most numerous unit of the <u>traffic police,</u> the DPS, except for a slight reduction in the number of individual officers.

The JIT units established in the Ministry of Internal Affairs system are unable to counter such criminal encroachments of traffic police inspectors on the rights of citizens as abuse of authority, fabrication of administrative materials and a number of other abuses.

The prosecutorial authorities and the system of the Investigative Committee of the Russian Federation ignore allegations of these types of offences.

Judges take the fabricated materials into consideration and, based on the results of their examination, issue indictments against the car owners.

In turn, judges legalise the criminal actions of traffic police inspectors by the convictions that have entered into legal force. All this causes a steady growth of corruption in the internal affairs bodies.

1.2. Attitudes of an average judge towards a motorist and a traffic police inspector: a comparative aspect

The main source of corruption is bias on the part of the judge. Communication with judges, their interviews and observations of judges' behaviour give grounds for the relevant conclusions. Let us compare the attitude of a judge towards a car owner and a traffic police inspector.

<u>**Attitude towards car owners:**</u>

:адменность: я ,удья, ты ;икто;

total summarisation of the :ravot of the police officer: if a protocol is drawn up, it means that the driver is guilty a priori;

-This is due to excessive workload; slowness of the judge in examining cases; lack of professional interest; orientation towards a higher judge, who is also not interested in following the procedures in examining cases and inevitably puts the ruling on hold;

deliberate issuance of an accusatory ruling so that, having learnt from bitter experience, the "owner" would next time "negotiate a "natural" agreement with the inspector;

recommendations, recommendations of an employee of the apparatus of a judicial district to a person brought to administrative responsibility to apply to a particular advocate's office (to a particular advocate) for the defence of his/her interests;

hints by the court- summoned inspector to hand over money to him in order to resolve the issue with the judge about the dismissal of the case in favour of the car owner.

The last case in practice is used very rarely. If the judge summoned the inspector to the consideration of the case, it means that the car owner proves the illegality of bringing to administrative responsibility, he considers himself innocent of the offence imputed to him and intends to act within the law. In addition, terminated proceedings on the case will spoil the performance indicators of the traffic police inspector.

<u>**Attitude towards traffic police inspectors:**</u>

unwillingness to spoil relations with the head of the district OGIBDD and subordinate traffic police inspectors;

reluctance to issue a lawful judgement in a case initiated at a corruption crossroads, because a later enforceable judgement may break the existing vicious practice, and therefore it is better to apply for any reason to issue an indictment;

Fear of claims from higher judges as to why the causes of the offences were not eliminated earlier;

fear of unlawful claims from higher judges about the allegedly "unjustified" release of "vtovladyetsya" from "deserved" punishments.

The ruling of the justice of the peace on the absence of corpus delicti and (or) events of an administrative offence in the actions of the driver can close the "trap of traffic police inspectors". The absence of a source of drawing up protocols will entail a decrease in performance indicators for traffic police inspectors. This will negatively affect their career and salary, as well as relations with the management of the unit. At the same time, traffic police inspectors, as well as some judges, will be deprived of the opportunity to use the situation for personal enrichment. The above criteria also apply to the work of a judge.

1.3. Recommendations on countering fabrication of an administrative offence case

None of mere mortals in Russia is immune from fabrication of a case of administrative offence against themselves. In recent years, fabrication of these cases has become a mass character. Malicious diminution of the rights of citizens by traffic police inspectors and judges, the increase in various abuses, the existing illegal law enforcement practice indicate the need to move away from the traditional and search for new effective ways to protect the rights of car owners. Despite the primitive nature of the current legislation, citizens are endowed with more opportunities to protect their rights and prosecute falsifiers than the latter to carry out administrative prosecution of citizens. However, it is necessary not only to know the laws, but also to be able to apply them in time. Doctors say: "The earlier you start treatment, the better your chances of staying alive". A similar principle applies in law.[13]

Consider what constitutes a fabricated case. **"Fabrication of a case" is the** *introduction of knowingly false information into official documents.*

Incorrect qualification of the actions of the car owner cannot be called fabrication of the case. If a real offence has been committed, then a case should definitely be initiated on this fact.

Various defence algorithms are constantly being improved. The suggested algorithm of actions of a car owner does not claim to be true.

We recommend beginners to be patient, to read the material carefully and, most importantly, to comprehend the readings. For a deeper understanding of the material, not only beginners, but even professionals, it is recommended to reinforce the read texts by studying the rules of law, which are contained at the end of the sentences.

For a novice who is not used to reading legal texts, this algorithm of actions may seem very complicated.

Always meet a traffic police inspector with audio and/or video recording equipment switched on. The recording should be made discreetly. When communicating with a traffic police inspector, it is necessary to be psychologically confident, polite, highly vigilant and, if necessary, act decisively.

In the case of unsubstantiated accusations under the switched on audio and (or) video recording device, repeat the duty phrases: **"I did not violate the rules, show me the evidence of my guilt"** and (or) **"If you want to accuse me, then acquaint me with the material evidence confirming my guilt".**

Not to fulfil unlawful demands to get out of the car and transfer to the patrol car for conversation (such an obligation is not imposed by the traffic rules). In 90% of cases cases on

---

[13] Shulipa Yu. Yu. How to ruin a fabricated case and stay with the rights? M - 2011. Moscow branch of FAR: http://www.far-msk.ru/?p=16155

administrative offences are initiated precisely after psychological treatment of the car owner in the patrol car. In this case, the victim syndrome is triggered, when the car owner, fulfilling the illegal requirements imposed on him, and at the same time, not providing proper mental resistance, gives reason to fabricate a case against himself.

If, despite the measures taken, the traffic police inspector started to draw up a report on the fact of not violating the traffic rules, it is necessary to do the following.

In the protocol on administrative offence immediately should be written duty phrases: **"I did not violate traffic rules of the Russian Federation, evidence of guilt is not presented, but fabricated. I ask to draw up a protocol only in the presence of my defence counsel. The rights provided by Art. 25.1 of the CAO and 51 of the Constitution of the Russian Federation are not explained to me",** additionally **"It is not clear to me what I signed for"** and nothing else. To make your arguments convincing, you should call 911, call the management of the territorial police department and take photos of the place of the incident. Subsequently, the collected evidence base will be useful for the investigation. More courageous, can write a statement in the form of explanation about the crime committed by the traffic police inspector and bringing the latter to criminal responsibility. Even more courageous can write this statement for hours, because the terms of writing statements for car owners are not limited by law. Such limitation is allowed only by federal law (part 3 of article 55 of the Constitution of the Russian Federation).

Such falsification of administrative materials is associated with abuse of official powers and the actions of the falsifier contain two offences under Art. 286 and Art. 292 of the Criminal Code of the Russian Federation. In order to prevent the DPS inspector from destroying the statement, it is necessary to write in the protocol that it is attached to the protocol.

If these preventive measures did not help and a protocol is drawn up, it is necessary to immediately take the initiative into their own hands. While the fabricated materials have not reached the magistrate, it is necessary to write and file a statement about the offence not later than 24 hours from the day of fabrication of the case to the commander of the traffic police unit: regiment, separate battalion, company in which the falsifier "works". This is one of the main conditions for preventing the hasty issuance of a ruling of indictment by a justice of the peace and detection of the committed offence.

It is worth noting that traffic police inspectors and justices of the peace, and for some categories of cases and federal - interact in a single organisational and legal relationship. This circumstance is a serious obstacle not only to an objective fair and impartial consideration of cases on administrative offences, but poses a more serious obstacle to the detection of committed offences.

Otherwise, if the justice of the peace issues an accusatory ruling, which on appeal to a higher court will remain in force, the **"legality" of the** actions of the traffic police inspector will be confirmed by a court ruling. Because of which it is virtually impossible to solve the committed offence later.

The statement should be motivated by the requirement to conduct a verification of the stated arguments and to send the statement together with the materials of the case on administrative offence as objects containing signs of crimes to the investigative department of the Investigative Committee of the Russian Federation.

In no case, it is impossible to let the case rest on its own and naively indulge in the illusion that the fabrication will be proved in court. The proverb that has entered the driving slang: **"As the inspector will sew the case, so the judge will judge",** has the right to the truth. In cases involving deprivation of the right to drive a vehicle, a protocol on an administrative offence is sent to the judge within three days from the moment of drawing up (part 1 of article 28.8 of the CAO RF).

The same amount of time is allotted for verification of a statement of offence and referral for investigation (paragraph 3 of part 1 of article 145 of the Code of Criminal Procedure of the Russian Federation).

Proceedings related to the movement of the statement about the crime are regulated by the instruction on the order of receipt, registration and resolution in the internal affairs bodies of the Russian Federation of statements, reports and other information about incidents (approved by Order of the Ministry of Internal Affairs of the Russian Federation of 4 May 2010 № 333).

Incoming incident reports, regardless of the place and time of occurrence, the completeness of the information contained therein and the form of presentation, are received round the clock at any internal affairs agency.

A report of an incident may be received by the internal affairs body personally from the applicant, by hand, by mail, by telephone, telegraph, public information systems, facsimile or other means of communication.

To receive messages in electronic form received via public information systems, software is used that requires the applicant to fill in the requisites necessary for handling incident reports.

The Internet message shall be printed out and further work with it shall be carried out as with a written message in accordance with the procedure established by this Instruction.

Reports of incidents received by the internal affairs agencies' records management and regime units by mail, by hand, by telegraph, by public information systems, by facsimile or by other means of communication shall be registered in accordance with the rules of records management and forwarded by the head of the internal affairs agency to the duty unit for immediate registration (p. 7-8).

Despite the fact that traffic police units do not maintain an independent CPCB (para. 15), the crime report is registered at the territorial IAB.

At the same time after registration of the crime report in the CPSS and referral for investigation, the necessary measures shall be taken to prevent or suppress the offence, as well as to preserve traces of the offence. The completed stub of the notification slip shall remain in the duty station (para. 19).

Before a criminal complaint is referred for investigation, the complaint shall be submitted to an official of the IAB, as a rule, vested with the rights of an inquirer.

If the inquirer within three days from the moment of registration of the statement about the offence in the CUSP did not send the statement to the investigative department of the Investigative Committee of the Investigative Committee of the Russian Federation, the inaction of the inquirer should be appealed against in accordance with Article 124 of the Code of Criminal Procedure of the Russian Federation.

Identical algorithm for appealing against unlawful actions (inaction) of an investigator of the investigative department of the Investigative Committee of the Investigative Committee of the Russian Federation in case of issuing a ruling on refusal to institute criminal proceedings, failure to consider an application (other actions and decisions).

The time limit for consideration of complaints under Article 124 of the Code of Criminal Procedure is three days. In exceptional cases, these time limits may be extended up to 10 days, of which the applicant is immediately notified. If the investigator (inquirer) has not considered the complaint within twenty-four hours, outside these time limits it is necessary to appeal against their actions in accordance with the procedure provided for in Article 124 of the CCrimP of Russia up to the Prosecutor General of the Russian Federation. If you do not receive a decision based on the law, you should complain about the actions (often inaction) of the Prosecutor General to the President of the Russian Federation.

In some categories of cases, the commander of a traffic police unit is not procedurally connected with inspectors, however, by virtue of the norms of departmental orders, he is obliged to exercise control over the activities of inspectors.

Commanders of regiments, separate battalions, companies should carry out inspections of traffic police units for compliance with discipline and legality, the established requirements in relations with road users, legality and completeness of initiation of cases on administrative offences *(p. 76 - 78.3 of the Instruction on the organisation of activities of* traffic *police units of the Ministry of Internal Affairs of the Russian Federation (approved by Order of the Ministry of Internal Affairs of the Russian Federation No. 186 of 02. 03. 2009 DSP)).*

During the period of verification of the arguments of the statement about the offence, the commander of the traffic police unit has no right to refer the case on an administrative offence to the court. Since the statement about the committed offence refers to the fabrication of administrative materials, it is impossible to verify the arguments of the statement separately from the fabricated case.

Submitting a criminal complaint to the commander of the DPS unit promptly informs him of the initiation of criminal prosecution of a subordinate.

In this regard, the commander of the traffic police unit is forced to postpone the transfer of the case to a justice of the peace for the duration of the inspection.

At the same time, as indicated below, the *commander of the DPS unit is not vested with the legal authority to refer cases on administrative offences to the court, which are within the exclusive competence of a judge*.

Thus, filing a statement about the committed offence to the commander of the relevant DSS unit is not only a way to take the initiative into their own hands, but also to prevent the fabricated case from reaching the magistrate.

According to p 23 of the Standard Regulations on the Uniform Procedure for Organisation of Receipt, Registration and Verification of Crime Reports (approved by Joint Order of the Prosecutor General's Office, Ministry of Internal Affairs, Ministry of Emergency Situations, Ministry of Justice, Federal Security Service, Ministry of Economic Development, Federal Drug Control Service of Russia No. 39/1070/1021/253/ 780/353/399 of 29.12.05), the duty officer on duty at the traffic police unit (traffic police department) is obliged to register the application in the KUSP and issue a notification coupon to the applicant.

Compliance with this rule means that the crime report is included in the state statistics, and it is no longer possible to get away with a formal response, as, for example, in the case of sending a crime report, bypassing the traffic police, to the investigative department of the Investigative Committee of the Investigative Committee of the Russian Federation.

If the commander of the traffic police unit did not ensure the registration in the CUSP and transfer of the statement about the crime with the materials of the fabricated case to the investigative department, it is necessary to immediately appeal against his illegal inaction to the superior and (or) the prosecutor in accordance with the procedure established by the Federal Law of 2 May 2006 N 59-FZ "On the procedure for consideration of appeals of citizens of the Russian Federation". It is possible, in addition, to file a statement to the territorial police department against the commander of the traffic police unit about the crime committed by him (part 1 of article 286 of the Criminal Code of the Russian Federation).

If the commander of a traffic police unit failed to ensure that the crime report was transferred to the investigative department of the Investigative Committee of the Russian Federation and sent the fabricated case to the court, such illegal action of the combatant should also be immediately appealed to his superior officer and (or) the prosecutor in the above-mentioned manner.

Before the justice of the peace accepts the case for proceedings, register in the office of the judicial district a petition to return the protocol together with the case to the <u>OGIBDD The</u> Supreme Court of the Russian Federation has clarified to all lower judges that a protocol that does not comply with Part 2 of Article 28.2 of the Code of Administrative Offences of the Russian Federation shall be returned for elimination of deficiencies.

Obviously, the fabricated protocol also contains fabricated information. Therefore, the fabricated protocol does not comply with part 2 of article 28.2 of the CAO RF. 2 of Article 28.2 of the CAO RF. The petition for the return of the protocol can be reconstructed into a petition for the return of the offence. It is worth attaching to the petition a copy of the notification ticket, informing in addition to the inconsistency of the protocol with part 2 of article 28.2 of the CAO RF that at the present time an inspection is conducted on the fact of fabrication of administrative materials in the manner prescribed by articles 141 - 144 of the Criminal Procedure Code of the RF.

If the justice of the peace accepted the fabricated case for production, it is necessary to immediately file a complaint against the illegal actions of the investigator (inquirer) in the production of which are verification materials in accordance with Art. 125 of the Criminal Procedure Code of the Russian Federation in the district court.

In parallel, it is worth appealing against illegal <u>actions of a justice of the</u> peace by filing written complaints to the chairmen of district and higher courts, regional qualification collegiums and councils of judges in accordance with the procedure established by the Federal Law of 2 May 2006 N 59-FZ "On the procedure for consideration of appeals of citizens of the Russian Federation". The drafting and sending of such complaints is not very difficult. It is only necessary to change the headings of the complaints. Complaints can be sent by registered mail with return notices to the addressee.

It should be noted that the judge's ruling as a procedural document is appealed in accordance with the procedure established by the CAO RF, together with the appealed final document - the ruling.

Therefore, it is necessary to put the subject of the complaint not the determination of the justice of the peace, but the actions of accepting the fabricated case for proceedings.

In response to question 16 of the Review of Legislation and Judicial Practice for the 4th quarter of 2008, the Supreme Court of the Russian Federation found that the analogy of procedural norms is permissible. Thus, the conduct of criminal proceedings is also a ground for suspending consideration of a case on an administrative offence. Using this circumstance, it is necessary to declare to the justice of the peace a motion to suspend consideration of the case until the entry into legal force of the ruling of the district judge. Then, after the suspension of consideration of the fabricated case, it is necessary to immediately write an application for termination of consideration of the complaint about illegal actions of the investigator (inquirer).

Consideration of the complaint in court deprives the opportunity to appeal against illegal actions in a more simplified and effective procedure under the administrative and prosecutorial line. In addition, if the complaint remains unsatisfied, the judge's ruling will become a reliable cover for the investigator (inquirer), and most importantly for the falsifier.

In order to suspend a newly reopened fabricated case, it is possible to reapply to the district court and so on until the expiry of the limitation period for bringing to administrative responsibility.

Thus, due to the absence of a number of procedural norms, the CAO RF is a simplified-punitive legislative act. Therefore, in addition to the CAO norms, in order to protect one's rights, it is necessary to fully use all procedures established by law.

Rarely any of the participants of administrative proceedings draws attention to the absence in the CAO RF of persons authorised by law to transfer a case on an administrative offence to the court, considered exclusively by a judge (justice of the peace). Let's conduct a brief normative analysis of the norms of CAO RF.

1) The traffic police inspector, who is an official, by virtue of para. 1 part 2 of Art. 2 part 2 of article 28.3 of the CAO RF initiates a case on an administrative offence, under the article entailing punishment only in the form of deprivation of the right to drive a vehicle for a certain period of time, belonging exclusively to the consideration of a justice of the peace. Immediately after the initiation of the case, the powers of the traffic police inspector end.

2) The case is considered only by a justice of the peace (part 1 of article 23.1 of the CAO RF).

Thus, from the moment of initiation of a case involving only deprivation of rights and up to the issuance of a ruling, two authorities are involved in the case: a traffic police inspector and a justice of the peace.

Which official of the traffic police unit is authorised by law to refer cases to the court?

In general, this category of cases is sent to the courts signed by commanders of traffic police units, their deputies, inspectors of administrative practice, and less often by chiefs of traffic police. Moreover, in the decision to refer the case to a justice of the peace, these officials refer to para. 2 part 2 of article 29.9 of the Code of Administrative Offences. 2 part 2 of article 29.9 of the CAO RF.

According to para. 2 part. According to paragraph 2 of part 2 of article 29.9 of the Code of *Administrative Offences of the* Russian Federation on the *results of consideration of a case about an administrative offence, a determination is made to transfer the case for consideration by jurisdiction, if it is found out that consideration of the case does not fall within the competence of the body, authority, official who considered it.*

However, commanders of traffic police units, their deputies, administrative practice inspectors, and chiefs of traffic police are not vested with the right to consider cases within the exclusive competence of justices of the peace.

By the way, the combatants themselves mention this circumstance in their responses to complaints against them, referring to part 1 of article 23.1 of the Code of Administrative Offences of the Russian Federation.

The analysis of the legislation confirms that the norms of the CAO RF do not give officials the right to transfer to the court cases on administrative offences that are in the exclusive competence of a justice of the peace (federal).

Often, instead of referral orders, sweeping letters are issued by unauthorised officials.

In the considered situation it is necessary to immediately appeal against illegal actions of a justice of the peace by filing written complaints to the chairmen of district and higher courts, regional qualification collegiums and councils of judges in accordance with the procedure established by the Federal Law of 2 May 2006 N 59-FZ "On the procedure for consideration of appeals of citizens of the Russian Federation". As stated above, drafting and sending such complaints is not very difficult, it is only necessary to change the caps.

In complaints it is necessary to raise the question on what grounds the court received the materials transferred by an unauthorised official and outside the procedure established by law?

In addition, similar complaints should be addressed to the district prosecutor and the superior head of the traffic police about the illegal actions of traffic police officials who illegally transferred the court case to the justice of the peace.

Before the court hearing, it is necessary to carefully study the materials and correctly determine the subject of proof of innocence. As a rule, the initial data disproving guilt are insufficient.

For this purpose, it is necessary to make motions to demand various evidences in the court session. For example, in order to establish the absence of a marking line on the road section indicated in the protocol, it is necessary to file a motion to demand the road traffic organisation project. To expose falsified readings of measuring devices, it is necessary to file a motion to demand their documentation.

The petition shall be subject to mandatory consideration by a judge, body, official in whose proceedings the case is pending (part 1 of article 24.4 of the CAO RF).

The petition shall be stated in writing and shall be subject to immediate consideration. A decision to refuse to satisfy a petition shall be made by a judge, body, official, in whose proceedings a case on an administrative offence is pending, in the form of a determination (part 1 of article 24.4 of the CAO RF).

In refusing to satisfy the petition, and, in fact, in demanding and (or) admission of materials as evidence, from paragraph 5 of part 1 of article 29.12 of the CAO RF follows from the judge's obligation to prove the reasons for his actions. 1 of Article 29.12(1) of the Code of Administrative Offences of the Russian Federation stems from the judge's obligation to motivate his actions with evidence.

The judge's refusal to grant one or a number of applications, for which it is impossible to prove innocence of the offence charged, without demanding the necessary materials, will inevitably lead to the issuance of a guilty verdict.

Therefore, if the judge unlawfully refused to satisfy the stated motions, it is necessary to challenge the judge on the grounds of obstructing the establishment of factual circumstances of legal significance in connection with the judge's being in unlawful collusion with the traffic police officers who have regular communication with the judge. The judge is obliged to give the necessary time for this.

Such behaviour of the judge will directly contradict the provisions of part 2 of article 26.2 of the CAO RF. The explanations of the person brought to responsibility, and together with them and the testimony of witnesses, as well as the evidence collected by the traffic police inspector in the protocol, have equal evidentiary value in the case and therefore cannot be disregarded on grounds not provided for by law. In other words, the grounds deliberately invented by the judge himself.

None of the evidence has a predetermined force. The evaluation of evidence is given by the judge on the basis of the results of consideration of the case and is contained in the ruling issued (Article 26.11 of the CAO RF).

The judge's inability to provide a reasoned documentary (evidentiary) refutation of the reasons for the recusal should be used as a repeated ground for a more severe recusal.

It is necessary, as well as communication with the traffic police inspector, to record the progress of the case on audio and (or) video recordings.

The current legislation of the Russian Federation does not contain a prohibition for persons participating in the open consideration of the case and citizens present in the court session to record the course of consideration of the case by means of audio recording.

Photography, video recording, broadcasting of open consideration of a case on an administrative offence on radio and television is allowed with the permission of a judge, body, official considering a case on an administrative offence (part 3 of article 24.3 of the CAO RF).

However, the CAO RF does not contain a direct prohibition on videotaping a court session. There is absolutely no liability for making a video recording of a court session without the judge's permission.

As practice shows, a video recording of a court session made without the judge's permission is used as evidence by the bodies of the judicial community and preliminary investigation.

After each trial, it is necessary to make a transcript of the proceedings on the basis of the audio and/or video recording made. Making a transcript starts with symbols. For example, L - Person in respect of whom - , MC - Justice of the Peace. Further phrases recorded in court are written in the transcript without abbreviations. An electronic medium of audio recording shall be attached to the transcript. Then, the transcript of the court hearing together with the electronic medium shall be attached to the case file upon written request. It is desirable to attach the transcript 3 - 4 days before the consideration of the case through the office of the justice of the peace. Such attachment will deprive the magistrate of the possibility to refuse to satisfy the stated motion. However, the law does not prohibit to attach the transcript in the course of consideration of the case.

Further, motions may refer to the information contained in the transcript as facts having evidentiary value in the case.

1.4. Tampering with evidence through deficiencies in the TCODD

In recent years, the formal attitude of the GIBDD leadership to the prevention of DTA, and the desire for formal and quantitative indicators of activity related to the detection of "offences" has led to the fact that the most "detectable offence" in the field of road traffic has become an offence under part 4 of article 12. 12. 15 of the CAO RF (driving in violation of traffic rules into the oncoming traffic lane). 15 of the Code of Administrative Offences of the Russian Federation (driving into the oncoming traffic lane in violation of traffic rules).

Every day, cases are initiated against hundreds of drivers under this norm. Where "offences" falling under the sanction of part 4 of article 12.15 of the Code of Administrative Offences are constantly committed, traffic police patrols are on duty almost around the clock. Moreover, the on-duty traffic police inspectors do not perform their duties to properly ensure traffic safety and the maximum possible prevention of violations of the rules, but only hide in the bushes from drivers' eyes, as if greedily hungry for drivers to commit offences. The consequence of such **police ambushes** is the mass transformation of uncooperative drivers into pedestrians for a period of 4 to 6 months by magistrates.

Let's consider variants of corrupt intersections where there is a high probability of driving on the oncoming lane, and not always connected with the violation of traffic rules:

;naks ;e comply with the requirements of technical standards;

signs are deliberately set up in such a way that their requirements contradict each other;

;nak ;ak is covered by a large-sized vehicle;

the markings are fully operational;

The markings are partially positioned in such a way that it is impossible to visually identify them;

-the markings are indistinguishable because of, neg, or dirt.

(U-turn (turn) on a small radius within an intersection.

Clause 1.3 of the RF Road Traffic Regulations states: Road users are obliged to know and comply with the requirements of the Regulations, traffic signals, signs and markings relating to them, as well as to comply with the orders of traffic controllers acting within the limits of the rights granted to them and regulating road traffic by the established signals.

Not every driver has the gift of telepathy, and traffic rules do not oblige drivers to be telepathic.

By literally enshrining these requirements, the legislature has placed duties on the driver to observe only those aforementioned roadside attributes that the driver physically can and should detect.

In other words, the driver is not obliged to comply with the requirements of traffic signals, signs and markings, if there are no such signals or if they are physically hidden from the driver's eyes by vegetation, large-sized vehicles, etc.

The grounds for the initiation of proceedings are the identified signs of guilt. Without guilt it is impossible to initiate a case. Since an administrative offence is always a guilty act (article 2.1 of the CAO RF).

The CAO RF establishes two forms of guilt: <u>intent</u> and <u>negligence</u> (Art. 2.2).

Physically not seeing a traffic light, sign, or markings it is impossible to foresee the possibility of harmful consequences of one's action (inaction).

In both cases, the existence of guilt is conditioned by the presence of physical and technical possibilities of the driver to foresee the occurrence of harmful consequences of his action.

In the cases in question, the driver physically cannot and should not foresee the possibility of the occurrence of harmful consequences of his action.

In this case, in the actions of the driver there are only external signs of an administrative offence. Such actions of the driver are Kazus.

CASUS - an <u>accidental action, which (unlike intentional or negligent) has external signs of an offence, but lacks the element of guilt and, therefore, does not entail legal liability</u>. In addition, the traffic rules of the Russian Federation do not impose on drivers the obligation to fulfil the requirements of road markings drawn in violation of GOST requirements.

Also, traffic regulations do not impose a duty on drivers to anticipate the presence of signs and markings where they do not physically exist.

There is another type of **"Traffic Police Trap,".** The road sign, which the motorist uses to guide his vehicle, contradicts the sign that follows it closely. For example, sign 3.1 "No Entry" is located several metres away from sign 4.1.1 "Going Straight" (e.g. Paveletskaya Square, Moscow, M. - 2010). Under such circumstances, the driver, often fulfilling the requirement of one road sign, inevitably violates the other nearby sign. Such situations can be found not only in alleys, but also on roads where the average speed of vehicles is usually around 90 km/h.

Let us consider whether in this case such an act is an administrative offence.

If the driver, complying with the requirement of one of the road signs forcedly violated a nearby established sign, then in view of the above circumstances by virtue of part 4 of article 1.5 of the CAO RF this act should be interpreted in favour of the driver.

In this situation, the following fact is irremovable doubt as to the driver's guilt:

<u>insufficient distance</u> between the road signs installed in violation of the requirements of GOST 52289-2004 due to which, complying with the requirement of one sign, the driver is <u>physically and technically</u> unable to prevent the violation of another. The driver is not physically and technically able to prevent the violation of another sign.

"To prevent physically" - to *detect in time the contradiction in the requirements, and to take measures up to the moment of detection up to the full stop of the vehicle, preventing the violation of the last sign.*

"Technically prevent" means the *technical ability of the vehicle to stop during the period . of .the moment the braking system is applied until it comes to a complete stop.*

(Given by analogy with the definitions: stopping distance and braking distance).

With regard to the second definition, we note that the braking distance of the vehicle also depends on the type of surface, as well as the condition of the road surface. When braking on asphalt pavement, the braking distance will be shorter than on icy road.

Under such circumstances, is bringing a person to administrative responsibility a fabrication of a case? Yes, it certainly is.

The easiest way to expose such fabrication is to use a video recording of the vehicle's route created with the help of a car recorder.

To unravel many fabrications, it is necessary to grasp such a seemingly simple concept as **"Oncoming Vehicle Lane".**

Road traffic rules are based on the provisions of the Constitution of the Russian Federation. Based on the provision of Part 3, Article 55 of the Constitution of the Russian Federation, everything that is not expressly prohibited by law is permitted. This principle is also directly applicable to traffic rules.

The Supreme Court of the Russian Federation has clarified that *under Parts 3 and 4 of Article 12.15 of the CAO RF should qualify directly prohibited by the PPP actions that are associated with the departure on the side of the carriageway, intended for oncoming traffic* (Resolution of the Plenum of the Supreme Court of the Russian Federation № 18 of 24 October 2006 On Some Issues Arising in the application of the Special Part of the CAO RF, as amended by Resolution of the Plenum of 11 November 2008 № 23).

This means that in places where driving into the oncoming lane is not expressly prohibited by the traffic rules, it is permitted.

However, due to the lack of a definition in the traffic rules of the Russian Federation on what is the **"Oncoming** lane", in pursuit of better performance, traffic police inspectors began to over-interpret the departure into the lane for oncoming traffic, bringing it almost under any violation of the rules.

The diversity of all traffic situations related to oncoming lane departure is not the subject of this paper. The main circumstances of driving into the oncoming lane are outlined above. As an example, let us consider the definition of the phrase **"Oncoming lane for the movement of vehicles",** given in one of the conclusions of a specialist on the case of an administrative offence and representing commonality for all cases of this category.

Question 1: Was the lane referred to in protocol 99 KA No. 1582036 and the ruling on the case of an administrative offence by the justice of the peace of the peace of the peace of the judicial district No. 96 of Moscow an oncoming lane for the movement of the car "Toyota-Avensis" driven by driver S. from a technical point of view?

Answer: the phrase "Oncoming traffic lane" is not precisely defined in the traffic rules, as well as in other regulatory legal acts of the Russian Federation, acting in the field of road safety, due to which various conflicts often arise when establishing the actual circumstances. Therefore, to answer the question, it is necessary to give a clear definition of the phrase "Oncoming traffic lane" and consider it in conjunction with the term "Intersection".

From the submitted materials of the case on administrative offence it follows that the accident in question occurred when completing the passage of the regulated intersection of Botanicheskaya Street - Stantsionnaya Street of Moscow, in the vicinity of the house 41a.

According to Clause 1.2 of the RF Traffic Code:

"Intersection" means a *place where roads intersect, join or branch at the same level, bounded by imaginary lines connecting respectively the opposite, most distant from the centre of the intersection, beginnings of carriageway roundabouts.*

The central part of an intersection consists of the intersection of carriageways. The carriageway intersection is always smaller in area than the intersection.

"Lane" means *any of the longitudinal lanes of the carriageway, marked or unmarked, and* *having a width sufficient for the movement of motor vehicles in a single lane.*

In S. I. Ozhegov's Dictionary of the Russian Language it is defined:

а) **"Windy"** - *moving to the ;rstretch;*

б) *"Movement"-moving someone-thing(s) (an object or its parts) in a <u>certain direction</u>:*

The movement of vehicles in the lane shall be rectilinear with respect to the lane limits in a single lane.

"Straight-line motion" is a mechanical motion in *which the displacement vector Gg does not change in direction and is equal in magnitude to the length of the path travelled by the body.*

$$|\Delta \vec{r}| = s$$

The totality of the above empirical evidence leads to the conclusion that: **"Oncoming vehicle lane" - a** *lane on which, contrary to the established mode of movement of vehicles, some vehicles move exclusively towards other vehicles . one row.*

<u>It does not follow</u> from the above-mentioned materials of the case on administrative offence <u>that when passing the intersection, the trajectory of the car</u> "Toyota-Avensis", under the control of driver C., <u>passes towards other vehicles in a strictly rectilinear direction.</u>

The initial data show that during the passage of the intersection, the lane referred to in the case materials as the **"Oncoming traffic lane",** was for the car "Toyota-Avensis", the **"Crossed traffic lane",** which passing the intersection of streets Botanicheskaya - Stantsionnaya in the area of 41a, the <u>car crossed at a certain angle in relation to the mode of traffic established on it.</u>

In addition, from the photographic materials of the case on administrative offence, it follows that the line of road markings 1.1 Annex 2 to the RF Traffic Rules from the side of Stantsionnaya Street in Moscow is located within the limits of the intersection in question.

This circumstance is of fundamental importance in assessing the driver's actions from a technical point of view, since within the intersection, the lane bypassing which he entered Stantsionnaya Street was not oncoming for him.

Conclusion: from a technical point of view, the lane referred to in the protocol 99 KA № 1582036 and the decision on administrative offence of the justice of the peace of the peace of the court site № 96 of Moscow as the oncoming lane for the movement of the car "Toyota-Avensis", GRZ "A 213 EB 199", under the control of driver S., is not[14] .

1.5. Detection of falsification of data on the presence of signs of alcohol intoxication

The available measuring instruments are far from perfect and do not exclude the possibility of inaccurate work, which is often abused by police officers and addiction psychiatrists to falsify evidence.

Let's reveal a couple of secrets about how some drug addicts and traffic police inspectors use their official positions to "turn" sober car owners into drunken alcoholics. Initially, if there are real reasons to believe that the driver is intoxicated, the traffic police inspector is obliged to suspend him from driving the vehicle and offer to undergo the so-called police examination (part 1.1 of article 27.2 of the Administrative Offences Code of the Russian Federation).

The requirements for the police alkotector and the procedure for its use are contained in paragraphs 5-8 of the Rules of examination of a person who drives a vehicle for alcohol intoxication and registration of its results, referral of this person for medical examination for intoxication, medical

---

[14] Additional conclusion of the specialist on the case about an administrative offence No. 71976 on part 4 of article. 12.15 of the CAO RF.

examination of this person for intoxication and registration of its results (approved by the Resolution of the Government of the Russian Federation of 26 June 2008 N 475) (as amended on 10 February 2011).

Based on these regulations, the police breathalyser:

a) technical means of measurement that provide a record of the results of the study on paper;

б) authorised for use by the Federal Service for Supervision of Health Care and Social Development;

в) verified in accordance with the established procedure by the Federal Agency for Technical Regulation and Metrology, the type of which is included in the State Register of Approved Types of Measuring Instruments (hereinafter referred to as technical measuring instruments).

Before alcohol intoxication examination, the traffic police inspector or VAL (if the driver of a vehicle belonging to the Ministry of Defence is detained) shall inform the testifying driver about the procedure of examination with the use of a technical measuring instrument, the integrity of the state verifier's stamp, the presence of a certificate of verification or a record of verification in the passport of the technical measuring instrument.

When conducting an alcohol intoxication examination, traffic police or traffic police inspectors shall be obliged to take a sample of exhaled air in accordance with the operating instructions of the technical measuring device used.

The presence or absence of alcohol intoxication shall be determined on the basis of the readings of the technical measuring instrument used, taking into account the permissible error of the technical measuring instrument.

The law imposes similar requirements on technical means.

Under special technical means are understood measuring devices approved in the established order as measuring instruments, having the appropriate certificates and having passed metrological verification (part 1 of article 26.8 of the Administrative Offences Code of the Russian Federation).

And based on the provision of part 3 of article 26.2 of the CAO RF it is not allowed to use evidence in a case on an administrative offence, obtained in violation of the law.

Other breathalysers, such as those purchased by traffic police inspectors at a flea market, which are not registered in traffic police registers and do not meet these criteria, are <u>outlawed and cannot be used</u>.

Blowing into a breathalyser in the cold is outlawed! Has anyone questioned the procedure of examination right in the cold? I think there are not many of them. But anyone blowing into the mouthpiece of the breathalyser in the cold not only runs a serious risk of getting sick for a long time, but also of being deprived of the right to drive a car for a long time. And regardless of whether he drank alcoholic beverages or not.[15]

In accordance with clause 2 of the operation manual of the ethanol vapour analyser ALKOTECTOR PRO-100:

- ambient air temperature range: 0 to 40 oC;
- relative humidity of ambient air not more than 95 %;
- atmospheric pressure range: 84.0 to 106.7 kPa.

The conclusion of FGU Penza CSM, states that alkotektors, modifications PRO-100 and PRO-100 combi, which are in service of traffic police inspectors should be operated in strictly provided for this temperature ranges - from 0 to + 40 degrees.

---

[15] Shulipa Yu. Winter exposure of the OCG of narcologists, traffic police and judges. M - 2011. Moscow branch of FAR: http://www.far-msk.ru/?p=17395

In sub-zero temperatures, the use of breathalysers is inadmissible.

In most regions of Russia, negative temperatures are holding more than positive. At the same time, a huge number of car owners underwent the so-called police examination right on the road. Now it is not difficult to understand what results such examinations have led to and, unfortunately, continue to lead to.

Paragraph 46 of the Administrative Regulations (approved by Order of the Ministry of Internal Affairs of the Russian Federation from 02. 03. 2009. № 185), states: "Technical means for traffic control, related to measuring devices, must be certified as a means of measurement, have a valid certificate of verification, issued by the Federal Agency for Technical Regulation and Metrology (kept in the unit), and be **used in accordance with the instructions and guidelines on the order of application of these means".**

Various deviations from the instructions and methodological guidelines for the use of technical means, including alcotecorders, are categorically inadmissible, as they lead to distorted results.

These circumstances fully apply to the conduct of medical examinations by psychiatrist-drug addiction specialists in mobile units (cars).

The requirements for a mobile station (vehicle) for medical examination for intoxication of persons who drive a vehicle (Annex N 9 to the Order of the Ministry of Health of the Russian Federation dated 14 July 2003 N 308 "On medical examination for intoxication") do not contain information about what air temperature should be inside the medical vehicle. Therefore, we are entitled to assume that the air temperature in the mobile medical vehicle is the same as outside.

Proving sub-zero air temperature is possible with:

a) certificates from the local department of Roshydromet about the air temperature during the period of certification;

б) technical information from the electronic thermometer.

It is advisable to stock up on the totality of this evidence before the next court hearing.

Among other things, the data on the air temperature at the time of the examination can be confirmed by a written report drawn up with the help of 2 or 3 citizens, who can be summoned to court as witnesses. It is also desirable to indicate the information about the air temperature in the protocol.

Those who have used medications not prohibited for driving are prescribed a repeat testing regime.

Let's remember that many motorists who have taken prescription drugs, under the influence of which driving is not prohibited, were illegally deprived of the right to drive. And the reason for such deprivations also lies in the improper use of alcotecgors.

According to clause 8.2.1. of the operating manual of the ethanol vapour analyser in exhaled air ALKOTECTOR PRO-100: "The analysed air sample must not contain particles of tobacco smoke, residues of ethanol or medicinal alcohol-containing preparations, as well as sputum and saliva, so it must pass before the test:

• at least 2 minutes after smoking;

• at least 20 minutes after consuming ethanol-containing drugs;

As alcohol is absorbed into the bloodstream, it may take 30 minutes after drinking an alcoholic beverage before it reaches its maximum concentration in the blood. This factor should be taken into account when analysing test results and prescribing a repeat test".

The Operation Manual of the ethanol vapour analyser ALKOTESTOR PRO-100 does not contain any prohibitions on the use of medical preparations containing ethanol by persons driving vehicles.

This product has been awarded the quality mark of medical equipment, and therefore, the ALKOTESTOR PRO-100 Breath Vapour Analyzer Operation Manual confirms the possibility of using medical preparations containing ethanol by persons driving vehicles. Special and repeated testing modes are provided for persons who have consumed medical preparations containing ethanol.

When was the last time, after you had consumed drugs, that a traffic police officer offered you a retest on their police breathalyser 30 minutes after the initial test?

When conducting a medical examination, paragraph 16 of the instruction on conducting a medical examination for intoxication of a person who drives a vehicle (Annex 3 to the order of the Ministry of Health of the Russian Federation from 14 July 2003 N 308) prescribes the following to narcologists.

The conclusion about intoxication as a result of alcohol consumption shall be made if the results of determination of alcohol in the exhaled air by one of the technical means of measurement carried out at an interval of 20 minutes are positive, or if at least two different technical means of indication for the presence of alcohol in the exhaled air are used, using both of them in each examination carried out at an interval of 20 minutes.

As is known, the body of any person contains a certain amount of endogenous alcohol in the blood (approximately up to 20 mg of alcohol in 100 g in combination with a complex of certain substances).

The legal limit of 0.3 ppm of alcohol in the body was introduced by federal law on 1 July 2008. However, these changes do not indicate that a driver is allowed to take a small amount of alcohol before getting behind the wheel.

Previously, the legislator, based on the methodology of endogenous alcohol content in the body, resulting from the use of certain non-alcoholic products and medicines, reasonably introduced this norm to separate alcoholics from those leading a sober lifestyle and to protect the latter from abuse by traffic police inspectors. In introducing these changes, the legislator was based on the vast experience of foreign countries.

For comparison, we note that the permissible dose of alcohol in the bodies of drivers in Belgium and Germany is 0.5 ppm, in France - 0.8, and in the USA - 1.0. At the same time, in these countries, drug addiction doctors bear serious responsibility for knowingly false medical opinion, as well as for violation of technologies (methods) of its conduction, and the procedures themselves are more transparent than in Russia.

Domestic practice shows that often during medical examinations, narcology doctors falsify the results of the examination to please the traffic police. In addition, drug addiction doctors do not always follow the examination technologies.

The frequent error of alcometres in conducting tests is also not taken into account. The use of alcometers with expired certificates of verification of devices or not included in the register of Gosstandart is noted.

Bringing guilty persons driving vehicles in a state of intoxication to deserved punishment, and innocent persons to exemption from responsibility is hindered by serious gaps in the current legislation on administrative offences and other normative acts, as well as their non-execution, or their execution only in a punitive aspect in violation of the established norms.

Medical examination for alcohol or drug intoxication is an expert examination, and the conclusion issued on its results is an expert opinion.

However, as the Supreme Court of the Russian Federation explained in its review of legislation and judicial practice of the Supreme Court of the Russian Federation for the fourth quarter of 2006 (answer to question 15), a narcologist (paramedic) conducting a medical examination of a driver's intoxication should not be warned of liability for giving a knowingly false opinion. In doing so, the Supreme Court referred to the fact that the Code of the Russian Federation on Administrative Offences does not provide for such a requirement.

This means that for giving a knowingly false opinion, an expert drug addiction doctor is not subject to administrative liability.

Only in extremely rare cases is it possible to bring a narcological doctor to disciplinary responsibility for giving a knowingly false opinion through higher regional medical institutions. This is hindered by medical corporatisation. In this regard, at the federal level there is a real need to change the legislation related to the establishment of criteria for the state of alcohol and drug intoxication of persons driving vehicles.

1.6. Detecting falsification of vehicle speeding data

Let us consider the basic fabrication of evidence on the example of the work of the most common speed measuring device "Vizir". The device has two main functions: video recording, functioning in the mode of "photofixation" *and* radar measurement. Both functions can operate in different modes.

Before operation, the device is set parameters: survey vector, permissible speed level, algorithm of object fixation. After that, the device itself detects vehicles travelling at excessive speed and informs about it by giving an audible signal. After that, it is enough to press the button of the device and the fixation of the speeding vehicle will take place. The information is given in the form of a small video clip or displayed in the form of a photo.

During the operation of speedometers, many "vigilant" traffic police inspectors identify their significant shortcomings, using them to fabricate incriminating evidence.

The "Visir" velocity meter has a number of standard drawbacks, admitted during development, which are inherent in all similar velocity meters. Let's consider the main drawbacks of this device.

1) Mismatch of geometric parameters of the radar meter and photo-video camera coverage area. The radar meter is technically capable of determining the speed of vehicles at a distance of 400 metres, while the photo-video camera can only record them at a distance of 80 metres. Because of this, the recorded speed may belong not to the vehicle that actually exceeded the speed limit, but to another vehicle that was following it ahead or behind.

2) When operating in the "Near Target" mode, the device detects a TC from which the radar meter detects a reflected signal of maximum power.

If the device operates in this mode and simultaneously aims at two objects (TCs), the target with the maximum reflective surface will be favoured.

3) When driving a patrol car, intentionally using "Stationary Mode" instead of "Patrol Mode" for the purpose of overestimating speed.

4) Due to unbalanced disproportional parameters of radar meter and photo-video camera operation, the speed of the fastest moving vehicle is detected in a dense flow, while the video camera records the closest vehicle to the device.

The accuracy of measurements is also affected by such factors as air temperature, sudden temperature changes, humidity, atmospheric pressure.

The easiest way to detect falsification of the cattle probe results is to use a navigator capable of recording route data or a tachograph.

1.7. Involvement of a specialist in the case

Nowadays the institute of participation of a specialist in proceedings on a case on an administrative offence is actively improving. Motorists have considerably more often started to involve specialists in the case.

Often, the detection of fraud in handwriting, metrology, traffic management and medicine requires specialised knowledge, which persons with higher professional education and experience in the relevant field possess.

Any adult person not interested in the outcome of the case and <u>possessing the knowledge</u> necessary to assist in the detection, fixation and seizure of evidence, as well as in the use of technical means (part 1 of article 25.8 of the Administrative Offences Code of the Russian Federation) may be engaged as a specialist. *The law does not establish a prohibition to summon a specialist to a court hearing on the initiative of the participants of the case.*

There are minimal requirements for a specialist. Higher professional education in the relevant field of knowledge and minimum work experience are sufficient. As a rule, judges rarely involve specialists in a case on their own initiative. Therefore, without waiting for the judge to issue a ruling of indictment, the parties to the case should on their own initiative involve a specialist.

It is advisable to involve specialists in the case after prior consultation.

Before contacting a specialist, it is necessary to photograph the case with a camera with a resolution of 8 to 12 megapixels (from cover to cover), for which purpose it is necessary to make a written request for familiarisation, specifying in it the make and model of the camera.

Then, send the received files together with the original copies of the documents to a specialist for examination.

The results of the conducted research are fixed by the specialist in the form of a written report.

The received expert's opinion shall be attached to the case, as well as the transcript of the court hearing on application through the court office, 2 - 3 days before the next court hearing.

Depending on the imputed act and the state of the case, the defence counsel, on his own initiative, should involve additional specialists in the case.

By the court hearing it is necessary to prepare a motivated motion to terminate proceedings on the case of an administrative offence, with references to the received evidence: the transcript of the previous trial and the conclusions of the expert handwriting expert and specialist, as well as the testimony of witnesses (if any were interviewed).

The CAO RF does not establish the ways of obtaining evidence from the sides of the defence counsel and the defendant, the victim and his representative. Therefore, the defence counsel has the right and obligation to collect evidence of innocence of the defendant by any lawful means.

Based on the provision of part 1 of article. 26.2. of the CAO RF evidence on a case of an administrative offence is any factual data, on the basis of which the judge, body, official, in whose proceedings the case is, establish the existence or absence of an event of an administrative offence, guilt of a person brought to administrative responsibility, as well as other circumstances relevant to the correct resolution of the case.

According to p. 18 of the Resolution of the Plenum of the Supreme Court of the Russian Federation № 24 of 24 March 2005, "On some issues of application of the general part of the CAO RF", when considering a case on an administrative offence, the evidence collected on the case should be evaluated in accordance with Article 26.11. of the CAO RF, as well as from the position of the law at their receipt (part 3 of Article 26.2. of the CAO RF).

Let's consider what kind of specialist should be involved in the case.

**POCHERKOVED.**

Before the court hearing, the defence counsel and the defendant should familiarise themselves with the case file. The presence of obvious forgery can be detected by comparing the information contained in the copy and the original protocol.

If there are forgeries in the case materials, for example: signatures of witnesses are forged, or persons not related to the case are included in the documents, or fictitious circumstances are added to the original documents to strengthen the accusation, the defence counsel (defendant) should, on his own initiative, initiate the involvement of a handwriting expert in the case.

TRAFFIC MANAGEMENT

The competent opinion of a traffic management specialist can also often help to make the judge pay attention to improper installation of signs and markings. An employee of a road maintenance organisation - the person responsible for the installation of road signs and road markings - or a lecturer from a motorway and road university can be invited to participate in the case as such an expert.[16]

TECHNICAL MEANS OF MEASUREMENT

In cases involving the use of technical measuring devices (Articles 12.8 and 12.9 of the Code of Administrative Offences of the Russian Federation), in order to give an opinion, the following documents of technical measuring devices, speed meters and alkotectors used by a traffic police inspector and a doctor-psychiatrist-drug addictionologist in full should be additionally requested from the OGIBDD at the stated request or on an initiative basis:
1. _Instrument Passport._
2. _Certificate of Conformity._
3. _Registration certificate with an appendix._
4. _Certificate of Measurement Type Approval with annex._
5. _Certificate of quality mark for medical equipment with (appendix (except for the gyrostemer)._
6. _Certificate of verification of the device._
7. _The operating manual of the device._
8. _Inventory card of the device._

NARCOLOGY

If a case on an administrative offence is initiated on the fact of detection of alcohol or drug intoxication of a person who drove a vehicle, a psychiatrist-narcologist working in a medical institution "independent" from the traffic police should be invited as a specialist. In case of distorted results of the alkotector it is necessary to additionally involve a specialist engineer in the field of metrology and standardisation.

In accordance with the orders of the Ministry of Health of the Russian Federation from 27 January 2006 № 40 "On the organisation of chemical-toxicological studies in the analytical diagnosis of the presence in the human body of alcohol, narcotic drugs, psychotropic and other toxic substances"; the Ministry of Health of the Russian Federation from 14 July 2003 N 308, from 14 July 2003 N 308 "On medical examination for intoxication", it is necessary to claim copies:
1. _Act of medical examination for intoxication of the person who drives the vehicle (Annex N1 to the Order of the Ministry of Health and Social Development of the Russian Federation from 14 June_

---

[16] Road traps have been placed on the Moscow map. ITAR-TASS /Interpress/M. 2011: http://www.firstnews.ru/news/lenta/20056/

2003 N308).

2. *Extracts from the journal of registration of selection of biological objects (Annex 52 5 to the Order of the Ministry of Health and Social Development2 of the Russian Federation from 27.01.2006 40).*

3. *Referrals for chemical-toxicological studies (Annex 20 7 to the Pr0x2y of the Ministry of Health 2 social27zvit00 2F 2t 27.01.200620 40).*

4. *Certificates of delivery of biological objects for chemical-toxicological (research (Annex 29 9 to the Order of the Ministry of Health and Social 2azvi1200 2F 2t 27.01.20062040).*

5. *Certificates on the results of chemical and toxicological studies (Annex 20 11 to the Order of the Ministry of Health and Social Development. Russian Federation from 27.01.2006 40).*

6. *Extracts from the journal of registration of chemical and toxicological studies (Annex 20 13 to the Order of the Ministry of Health and Social Development 2F 27 27.01.2006 242 40).*

The person brought to administrative responsibility must submit certificates from attending physicians on the presence of relevant diseases and on the use of relevant drugs in this regard (if any).

By examining the data contained in the above materials in their interrelation, an independent specialist psychiatrist-drug addiction doctor can come to a reasonable conclusion about obtaining the results of drug intoxication due to the use by the car owner of drugs not contraindicated for use while driving, or about the violation of medical technology of obtaining the results of the examination.

CHAPTER 2

JUDICIAL MONITORING

2.1. Public control over the activities of traffic police

The legal provision of public control is of constitutional importance.

Based on the provision of part 3 of article 55 of the Constitution of the Russian Federation, human and civil rights and freedoms may be restricted by federal law only to the extent necessary to protect the foundations of the constitutional order, morality, health, rights and legitimate interests of other persons, to ensure national defence and security of the state.

In other words, everything that is not expressly prohibited by federal law is subject to public control.

Public control is carried out by representatives of public associations, as a rule, to achieve the goals of statutory activities, and by individual citizens.

In this manual, **"public representatives"** *and (or) "members of the public" are members of public associations, groups of citizens exercising public control over the activities of public authorities.*

Citizen patrols and judicial monitoring in the field of road traffic are interrelated and interdependent types of public control. Therefore, it is not possible to consider these two phenomena in isolation from each other.

Without a civilian patrol, judicial monitoring cannot be fully carried out.

Public control over the activities of traffic police inspectors in the street and road network is carried out in the form of a civil patrol.

In S. I. Ozhegov's Dictionary of the Russian Language it is established **"Patrol"** *(French patrouille) - a small group of a military unit, militia, to monitor order, security in a certain area.* [17]

"Citizen patrol" differs from "patrol" in the classical sense in that the observation of order and security in police activities is *carried out by citizens.*

Let's define this emerging term.

"Civil Patrol" *a type of public control carried out by representatives of public associations, a group of independent citizens over the activities of units of internal affairs bodies, traffic police, road maintenance and road construction organisations, with the help of audio and video recording means.*

The basic principles of civilian patrols in the street and road network, including fixed posts, are stealth, discreetness and professionalism.

The principle of secrecy consists in carrying out public control without publicity and reporting about it to a wide range of persons. Only the results of control measures are subject to public disclosure, not information about their implementation.

The principle of invisibility consists in exercising public control in such a way that traffic police inspectors are unable to notice the observation of the public in their activities.

The principle of professionalism consists in the knowledge of public representatives of the current legislation in the field of road safety and the practice of its application, in their professional possession of technical means of audio and video recording, in their possession of skills of operative-search and counterintelligence activities, mobility and efficiency.

Members of the public should have high moral qualities, good psycho-physiological training, be disciplined and vigilant, act decisively, courageously and persistently, and endure the difficulties associated with the implementation of control. In dealing with traffic police inspectors, they should

---

[17] Ozhegov S. I. Dictionary of the Russian Language, M. - 2007. Onyx and Education, p. 637.

be polite and tactful, and their actions should not go beyond the current legislation of the Russian Federation.

In order to ensure their own safety and to achieve the effectiveness of the control measure, public control should be carried out by a group of citizens.

As a rule, the places of public control in the street and road network are corrupted intersections. Less often they are fixed posts of traffic police *and* checkpoints.

The phrase **"Corruption Crossroads"** can be given three definitions:

1) *a road section, on which, due to improper installation of signs, markings and their operation, complex geometric configuration of the roadway, other road conditions, drivers commit random actions that have signs of an offence, but lack the elements of the law, which traffic police inspectors deliberately use to increase their performance and take money from drivers;*

2) *a road section where, due to improper installation of signs, markings and their operation, complex geometric configuration of the roadway, other road conditions, drivers unintentionally commit mass administrative offences, which are used by traffic police inspectors to increase their business opportunities, to take money from drivers;*

3) *a road section where traffic police inspectors deliberately distort the results of technical measuring devices, as well as perform other illegal actions in order to increase their performance and take money from drivers.*

In fact, countering the collusion of traffic <u>police</u> and courts is a complex public activity of a reconnaissance and search nature, directly related to penetrating into the intentions of traffic police inspectors (traffic police), justices of the peace and federal judges in order to obtain information about committed or impending unlawful acts against car owners.[18]

Public control over the activities of traffic police inspectors should be carried out as secretly as possible. Public controllers should develop an agreed action plan in advance and distribute control responsibilities among themselves. The form and technology of the control activity should be chosen depending on the specific situation.

The practice of public control shows that if traffic police inspectors detect visual observation of their activities, they contact the department duty officer and then suddenly leave their seats.[19]

For example, if the corrupt intersection is located outside the city in the forest, it is necessary to hide cars in the nearest bushes and monitor them from the forest.

Community monitors can control the activities of traffic police officers by dressing up in road workers' uniforms, imitating cleaning the carriageway or checking road conditions, imitating passengers waiting for a bus, or advertising agents of a commercial organisation.

If the corrupt intersection is located in an open area near markets, large transport interchanges, or car parks for heavy vehicles, the community watchdog can change into a work uniform, take a poster of the commercial organisation's services, and record video through it. This unobtrusive type of surveillance will give the opportunity to get as close as possible to the traffic police and make not only a clearer video recording, but also an audio recording of the events. This type of control will undoubtedly increase its effectiveness. In the course of monitoring, in order to be reinsured against possible illegal actions of the police, the public observer who monitors the activities of traffic police inspectors should be under constant supervision of his colleagues.

---

[18] Shulipa Y. Y. Technology of counteraction to unlawful collusion of traffic police and courts. M. - 2011. Moscow branch of FAR: http://www.far-msk.ru/?p=13563

[19] NTV story about the "trap" at Paveletskiy railway station from 03 July 2010: http://www.youtube.com/watch?v=LD94X0zTyz8

Video recording of the activities of traffic police inspectors should be carried out continuously until they detain car owners. After the detention, the public controller should focus on recording the communication between the car owner and the traffic police inspector and drawing up protocols.

At the end of communication between a traffic police inspector and a motorist, the recording controller should immediately inform his/her colleague.

After the car owner and the traffic police inspector have separated at a sufficient distance, the colleague of the public inspector should approach the car owner, introduce himself, give the name of the public organisation and the purpose of the event. Also to inform about the video recording, which the public controllers intend to submit to the court hearing as evidence refuting the guilt of the car owner. Subsequently, after studying the accusatory materials and the video recording of the events, the representatives of the public, the car owner and his defence counsel should develop a position on the case. It is recommended to send the recording made with a complaint about the illegal actions of the traffic police inspector to the prosecutor's office, and (or) if there are signs of crime in his actions, to the investigative authorities.

It should be noted that the form of public control over the activities of DSS conducted at the same corruption intersection should not be the same.

Subsequently, when a complaint is filed, the management of the traffic police inspector will notify him or her of the video recording. The traffic police inspector can also find out about it through a justice of the peace.

It is therefore recommended that the video recording of the events be presented to the judge and that members of the public be interviewed as witnesses only after the traffic police inspector has been interviewed.

Once the traffic police inspector is aware of the control measures taken against him, he will henceforth behave with extreme caution at that intersection, or he will be redeployed to another duty station.

2.2. Global monitoring tactics

One of the important circumstances contributing to the exposure of unlawful collusion is the study and generalisation of court decisions on the websites of the Russian courts based on the results of the consideration of specific cases.

In a broad sense, **"Judicial monitoring" is a** *type of public control over the activities of the judiciary.*

Judicial monitoring is divided into two types: **Global** and **Local.**

Global monitoring - *observation and collection of information from the official websites of the courts of the Russian Federation, periodic information and legal sources on judicial acts issued by the courts of the Russian Federation and judicial community bodies, their generalisation and legal analysis, as well as personnel movements of judges.*

Local monitoring - *observation and collection of information on legally significant actions of a judge or a panel of judges, bodies of the judicial community in the course of their consideration of specific cases and performance of their professional activities.*

Members of the public are familiar with the locations of corrupt intersections and, as a rule, the time of deployment of traffic police units at them.

Representatives of public associations receive this information based on the results of monitoring of judicial acts on the Internet, from the reports of trapped car owners on the Internet forums, with the help of their agents - current traffic police inspectors and heads of their departments.

It is worth noting that some members of the public are former traffic police inspectors, or in one way or another were previously associated with the activities of the traffic police. They have a real opportunity to receive from their former colleagues internal documents: cards of the post, patrol route of the inspector (p. 39 of the order of the Ministry of Internal Affairs of the Russian Federation of 2.03.09, No. 186 dsp); job descriptions of specific inspectors (p. 15 of the order of the Ministry of Internal Affairs of the Russian Federation of 2.03.09, No. 186 dsp), information about technical means of measurement, personal qualities of individual employees, information about the place and time of deployment of traffic police units.

In addition, on the basis of articles 8 and 27 of Federal Act No. 149 of 27 July 2006 on information, information technologies and the protection of information and Act No. 82 of 19 May 1995 on voluntary associations, voluntary associations may request the information in full. The internal affairs bodies have no right to refuse to provide this information.

One of the important circumstances contributing to the exposure of unlawful collusion is the study and summarisation of court decisions on the websites of Russian courts based on the results of the consideration of specific cases.

By virtue of part 2 of article 15 of the Federal Law of 22. 12. 2008г. N 262-FZ "On Ensuring Access to Information on the Activities of Courts in the Russian Federation" - the texts of judicial acts subject to publication in accordance with the law, as well as the texts of other judicial acts issued by the Constitutional Court of the Russian Federation, constitutional (statutory) courts of the constituent entities of the Russian Federation, arbitration courts, with the exception of the texts of judicial acts specified in part 4 of this article, are posted on the Internet in full.

As is known, the ruling on the case of an administrative offence must specify:

1. *official, surname, name, patronymic of the judge, official, name and composition of the collegial body that issued the ruling, their address;*
2. *date and place of consideration of the case;*
3. *information about the person in respect of whom the case was considered;*
4. *the circumstances established during the examination of the case;*
5. *article of the present Code or law of the subject of the Russian Federation, providing for administrative responsibility for committing an administrative offence, or the grounds for termination of proceedings on the case;*
6. *a reasoned decision on the case;*
7. *the term and procedure for appealing against the ruling* (part 1 of article 29.4. of the CAO RF).

The overall results of civil patrols and court monitoring can reveal that the number of vehicles stopped for traffic violations by drivers does not correspond to the number of cases initiated and subsequently considered.

For example, according to the results of observations of the members of the Moscow branch of the FAR over the activities of inspectors of the 3 BPS of the traffic police of the Central Administrative District of Moscow, out of 20 motorists detained on suspicion of violating traffic rules, protocols on administrative offences were drawn up on average only in respect of 2 persons.[20]

At the same time, in the specified period the number of cases received by the 3 BPS of the traffic police of the Central Administrative District of Moscow under part 4 of article 12.15 of the CAO RF is higher than the number of rulings issued by the justice of the peace of the peace of judicial district

---

[20] Shulipa Yu. Yu. Diagnostics of Moscow administrative justice. The first results on the example of corruption crossroads - Paveletskaya Square, Moscow. Moscow. Scientific and practical report. M-2010. Moscow branch of FAR: http://www.far-msk.ru/?page_id=11241

No. 102 of Moscow based on the results of their consideration.[21]

This type of control can be exercised through requests to the heads of DSS units and the presidents of the relevant courts.

The above-mentioned legal provisions allow public associations to receive this information in full without any restrictions or prohibitions.

Systematising this information will help to identify common patterns. On the basis of this information, a general and specific timetable for the initiation of cases should be created. The general schedule should be based on information about the appearance and disappearance of corruption crossroads within one region, their number, and the volume of cases initiated under the articles of the Code of Administrative Offences over the last six months.

Individual schedules should be developed for each specific corruption junction. They should include information on the number of cases initiated under the relevant articles of the Code of Administrative Offences during the day and the time of committing the imputed acts.

Such systematisation of the data obtained will provide the most complete information on the location of corrupt intersections and the time of deployment of traffic police units at them, as well as on the substance of the imputed acts.

2.3. Local monitoring tactics

In courts, the tasks of public representatives are to collect complete information on legally significant actions of a judge, or a panel of judges, or the bodies of the judicial community.

These tasks can be solved only in the course of their consideration of specific cases: criminal, administrative, civil, disciplinary, i.e. during the professional activities of judges or members of the judicial community.

Public control over the judge's actions begins even before the start of the consideration of the case in the courthouse. Often in Russian courts the consideration of cases starts with traditional delays of several minutes to hours.

It is the responsibility of the judge to decide on the appointment of the time and place of consideration of the case (para. 1 part 1 of Article 29.4 of the CAO RF). This means that the consideration of the case must begin exactly at the appointed time.

If, after waiting for thirty minutes, the scheduled hearing of the case has not started due to the absence of the judge, the persons involved in the case and members of the public should draw up a record of the judge's absence from his or her workplace. If the judge is present in the court building, but ignores the hearing of the case at the appointed time, a statement of failure to hear the case at the appointed time should be drawn up.

The act is drawn up in a free written form addressed to the chairman of the district (city) court and serves to establish a legal fact - failure to consider the case by the judge at the appointed time. The act shall specify the surnames, first names, patronymics, signatories, their addresses and, if desired, other contact details.

The act shall be drawn up in at least two copies, one of which shall remain in the hands of one of the applicants.

After drawing up the act, the act must be immediately handed over and registered in the clerk's office of the district (city) court.

Under such circumstances, if the judge decides to hold a meeting later at a different time and in

---

[21] Voyevodin V. A. Paveletskaya - continuation of history. M-2010. Moscow branch of FAR: http://www.far-msk.ru/?p=7849

the absence of participants in the proceedings, then on appeal the ruling shall be cancelled by the judge of a higher court as issued with a significant violation of procedural norms (para. 4 part 1 of article. 30.7 of the CAO RF), and the case shall be sent for a new consideration. If the statute of limitations for bringing to administrative responsibility has expired (and para. 6 part 1 of article. 24.5 of the CAO RF), the judge of a higher court, guided by para. 3 ч. 1 part 1 of article 30.7 of the CAO RF is obliged to cancel the decision, and to stop proceedings on the case.

Practice shows that during consideration of cases on administrative offences not every judge ensures that the record of the court session is kept.

For example, in Moscow, even if defence lawyers or persons involved in the case file appropriate motions, justices of the peace and federal judges refuse to keep records of court hearings on spurious grounds. On the contrary, justices of the peace and federal judges of the Moscow Region, by order of the Presidium of the Moscow Regional Court, ensure the maintenance of records of court hearings.

However, keeping a record does not mean recording in it the correctness and completeness of all legally relevant circumstances revealed during the consideration of the case.

When considering a case on an administrative offence, the person in respect of whom the case has been initiated and his/her defence counsel shall invite in advance to the court session representatives of the public.

As noted above, members of the public should have knowledge of the law, tactical experience in exercising public control over the activities of the courts and the conduct of court hearings, and the ability to professionally use technical means of audio and video recording.

It should be noted that the current procedural legislation of the Russian Federation does not contain a prohibition for persons participating in the open consideration of the case and citizens present in the court session to record the course of consideration of the case by means of audio recording.

Photography, video recording, broadcasting of open consideration of a case on an administrative offence on radio and television is allowed with the permission of a judge, body, official considering a case on an administrative offence (part 3 of article 24.3 of the CAO RF).

However, the CAO RF does not contain a direct prohibition on videotaping a court session. There is absolutely no liability for making a video recording of a court session without the judge's permission.

As practice shows, a video recording of a court session made without the judge's permission is used as evidence by the bodies of the judicial community and preliminary investigation.

Recommendations on the use of a dictaphone in court hearings are minimal and depend on the degree of falsification of the case, the corruption of the DSS inspector being questioned, and the adequacy and dependence of the judge hearing the case.

Compared to using a video camera, using a voice recorder is somewhat easier and is done in reverse order.

If the case is clearly fabricated, during the trial the traffic police inspector is questioned, the judge behaves inadequately, communicates with the participants in a dismissive manner, belittles the honour and dignity of the citizens present, prevents the application of motions, imposes on the participants duties not provided for by law, deliberately disrupts the course of consideration of the case, it is better to record the trial on a tape recorder and (or) video camera secretly.

It makes no sense for the defence counsel and the defendant to object to such unlawful actions of the judge. Even after defence counsel's objections, a judge with such a deliberately biased attitude may continue to disregard the law.

However, the material evidence obtained with the help of a dictaphone and (or) video camera will serve as a basis for cancellation of an unjust judicial act.

If it is known that the judge considering the case does not suffer from accusatory-punitive bias and has no sympathy for traffic police inspectors, the dictaphone recording can be carried out openly by placing the dictaphone on the table.

In the case of covert audio recording, it is recommended to place the recorder in the pocket of outer clothing. The main thing is that a thick layer of clothing should not cover the microphone. If the outer clothing consists of a thin layer, the recorder can be safely disguised in any pocket.

The dictaphone as well as the video camera must be switched on after the secretary has been summoned to the court session.

It is more effective to record the course of the case with the help of a hidden video camera. It is well known that judges and traffic police inspectors are extremely sensitive to publicity of their illegal actions. Subsequently, the made video recording can be sent to the bodies of the judicial community to address the issue of bringing the judge to disciplinary responsibility, reproduced in the media and posted on the Internet for wide access, serve as a basis for cancellation of the judicial oppression under appeal.

As a rule, in the course of court proceedings, the defence counsel and the person brought to administrative responsibility, operate with a large number of materials: copies of case sheets, documents, petitions. Often it is necessary to prepare motions directly during consideration of the case.

Unlike the use of a dictaphone, it is practically impossible for a defence counsel to make a full-fledged video recording of a court session.

Therefore, the videotaping of the trial should be entrusted to a member of the public.

Before the start of the court session, the technology of video recording should be agreed with the defence counsel and agreed with a member of the public.

In view of videotaping the trial, it is necessary to decide on the positioning of the persons present at the hearing so that the persons involved in the case and the judge are in the field of view of the lens.

When making video recordings, such important circumstances as the size of the courtroom, the lighting of the room, the location of the presiding officer's table and seats for those present in the court session, and the technical parameters of the video camera must be taken into account.

Ideally, in order to ensure the quality of evidence, a member of the public should make a video recording so that the statements of each person involved in the case are recorded in full. The footage should include the exhibits presented in court and the judge's examination of the case file.

A member of the public shall closely follow the proceedings and, after the judge has spoken to the person involved in the case, shall discreetly redirect the lens to the person speaking.

It is desirable to have two members of the public videotape the court session, simultaneously from two video cameras.

If the presiding officer and (or) the bailiff discover that the court proceedings are being secretly video-recorded, the judge shall have the right to prohibit a member of the public from video-recording. If the public representative does not stop videotaping, he/she may be removed from the courtroom by the judge's decision.

In case of removal of a public activist, it is recommended to find a reason for postponement of the case. Postponement of the case will temporarily suspend the unlawful actions of the judge, will help the defence and public activists, taking into account previous mistakes, to better prepare for the next hearing.

Maintaining dual video recordings will provide the public with mutual insurance and facilitate better and more complete collection of evidence obtained at trial.

After the trial, the defence counsel and the defendant should carefully review the audio and/or video recording. The recording of the court hearing will reveal possible mistakes made by the defendant, defence counsel, judge, witnesses and other participants in the case, which may affect the judgement, which will subsequently help to improve defence tactics.

From the video recording, an audio recording should be recorded on electronic media for later admission into evidence.

A written transcript of the court hearing must be made on the basis of the recording, an electronic audio recording medium must be attached to the transcript, and the transcript must be attached to the case file upon written request by the court office. The transcript together with the electronic carrier may also be attached to the case file during the next court hearing by submitting a written application to that effect. However, if the judge is incurably suffering from an accusatory-punitive bias, he or she may refuse such a request on spurious grounds.

The judge has no right to refuse to satisfy the application. Therefore, the option of attaching the transcript of the court hearing and the electronic media to the case file via the court office is the safest.

After each consideration of a case, if there are signs of disciplinary offence in the actions of a judge, it is necessary to immediately draw up complaints to the chairmen of district (city) regional courts - the CCJ and the Council of Judges, only changing the headings of the complaints.

Before the court hearing, the defence counsel and the defendant must familiarise themselves with the case file. If there are forgeries in the case materials, for example: signatures of witnesses are forged, or persons not related to the case are included in the documents, or fictitious circumstances are added to the original documents to strengthen the prosecution, the defence counsel should initiate a handwriting expert examination of the materials on his own initiative. For this purpose, it is quite enough to photograph the case with a camera with a resolution of 8 to 12 megapixels and send the obtained files for comparative study to a handwriting expert.

Before familiarising yourself with the case, you must make a written request for familiarisation, specifying the make and model of the camera.

The obtained expert report should be attached to the case as well as the transcript of the court hearing through the court office 2 - 3 days before the next court hearing.

Depending on the imputed act and the state of the case, the defence counsel, on his own initiative, should involve additional specialists in the case.

For the court hearing it is necessary to prepare a motivated motion to terminate proceedings on the case of an administrative offence, with references to previously obtained evidence: the transcript of the previous trial and the conclusions of the expert scribe and specialist, as well as the testimony of witnesses (if any were interviewed).

<u>CAO RF does not establish the ways of obtaining evidence from the sides of the defence counsel and the defendant, the victim and his representative.</u> Therefore, the defence counsel has the right and obligation to collect evidence of innocence of the defendant by any lawful means.

Based on the provision of part 1 of article. 26.2. of the CAO RF evidence on a case of an administrative offence is any factual data, on the basis of which the judge, body, official, in whose proceedings the case is, establish the existence or absence of an event of an administrative offence, guilt of a person brought to administrative responsibility, as well as other circumstances relevant to the correct resolution of the case.

According to p. 18 of the Resolution of the Plenum of the Supreme Court of the Russian Federation № 24 of 24 March 2005, "On some issues of application of the general part of the CAO RF", when considering a case on an administrative offence, the evidence collected on the case should be evaluated in accordance with Article 26.11. of the CAO RF, as well as from the position of the law at their receipt (part 3 of Article 26.2. of the CAO RF).

The main thing is that the evidence presented by the defence counsel should be consistent with each other in a logical sequence. For this purpose, it is necessary to indicate in the application for admission of the obtained evidence the sources, place, time and technical means of their obtaining. In the theory of law and the practice of law enforcement there is a presumption of good faith. In other words, every item is presumed to be genuine, true and valid until proven otherwise. Therefore, the burden of proving the invalidity of the evidence presented by the defence is, by default, on the judge.

Often in law enforcement practice there are cases when judges unreasonably refuse to satisfy such petitions. It is this circumstance that gives sufficient grounds to assume that the traffic police inspector and the judge are in unlawful collusion.

The decision to refuse to satisfy the petition shall be made in the form of a ruling (part 2 of article 24.4. of the CAO RF). The ruling must specify the circumstances established during the consideration of the petition, case materials and set out the reasons on which the court came to the relevant conclusions (paragraph 5, part 1, article 29.12. of the CAO RF). But how can such a ruling set out the real reasons, when the evidence presented by the defence counsel does not indicate otherwise? No evidence can have a predetermined force (Art. 26.11. of the CAO RF).

So, in such cases, the judge deliberately invents motives to avoid examining evidence that is undesirable to him and the traffic police inspector.

Thus, by his unlawful actions, through the use of his official position, the judge rejects the evidence presented by the defence counsel in advance without proper examination, deliberately depriving them of legal force. These circumstances show that the judge is avoiding in every possible way to make a ruling based on the law.

Under such circumstances, during the hearing of the case, the defence counsel and (or) the defendant should make a strongly motivated challenge to the judge on the grounds of being in unlawful collusion with the traffic police inspector who prepared the accusatory materials. The likelihood of such a challenge being granted is negligible.

However, as law enforcement practice shows, when reviewing indictments, higher judges take into account the position of defence counsel's challenge and often annul indictments on this basis alone.

Specialised public associations and individual citizens should post on the relevant thematic Internet resources legal and justified court rulings and decisions that have entered into force.

It is well known that the representatives of the Themis do not make mental and physical efforts when considering cases, they tend to rewrite from the record the accusation's fabula and on its basis make an accusatory ruling.[22]

In this regard, it is recommended that, in the course of court proceedings, the judge be familiarised with judicial acts in similar cases that have entered into legal force.

A lawful and well-founded ruling (decision) of a court in a similar case that has entered into legal force contributes to the correct application of the law by the court in a similar case and creates the effect of procedural time saving.

It should be noted that this method of obtaining a lawful judicial act is not always effective. The author notes that in the regions of the country there are different law enforcement practices that are

---

[22] Shulipa Yu. Arbitrariness of traffic police and courts. According to the materials of the press conference on 1 December 2010. M-2010. Moscow branch of FAR: http://www.far-msk.ru/?p=10594

rooted at the level of presidiums of regional courts.[23]

It is known that when considering any case, the court interprets the legislation. This type of interpretation in the theory of law is called casual interpretation. Casual interpretation is carried out only by a law enforcement body on a particular case and is relevant to a particular case. Nevertheless, court rulings (decisions) that have entered into legal force have the force of law and, from the point of view of uniformity of judicial practice, prescribe that other judges and officials of executive authorities should be guided by the legal position expressed in earlier judicial acts.

2.4 Utilisation of global monitoring results

Despite the common nature of public monitoring, global and local monitoring have differences in their goals and objectives.

As is known, the ultimate goal of judicial monitoring is to strengthen law and order in the activities of traffic police and courts, to properly ensure the protection of the rights and legitimate interests of citizens in the field of road traffic, and to establish civil society and the rule of law.

If on the basis of the materials received in the course of public control, a justice of the peace terminates proceedings on cases of administrative offences, or a judge of a district (city) court cancels convictions, then, on the basis of the judicial acts that have entered into legal force, a public association should apply to the prosecutor's office of the subject of the Russian Federation with a petition to bring a protest against earlier unjust judicial judicial acts.

According to part 3 of article 30.12. of the CAO RF the right to bring a protest in the order of supervision belongs to prosecutors of subjects of the Russian Federation and their deputies, the Prosecutor General of the Russian Federation and his deputies. The norms of the CAO do not establish the term for bringing a protest against judicial acts on the case of an administrative offence that have entered into legal force. A public association may also be the initiator of an appeal to the regional prosecutor to bring a protest against judicial acts that have entered into legal force.

In order to normalise the road transport process, eliminate corruption and various abuses in the street and road network, it is necessary to address the heads of road maintenance services to eliminate various shortcomings in the TIACS. In case the heads of road maintenance services do not take action to eliminate deficiencies in the TIACS, it is necessary to immediately appeal against their unlawful inaction in accordance with the established procedure. It is possible to make proposals to the authorities to improve road traffic.

In addition to initiating various legal procedures, the results of local monitoring may lead to appeals to the manufacturers of technical measuring devices to eliminate deficiencies in the operation of the devices, leading to various abuses by police officers and psychiatrists-drug addicts who use them to falsify evidence.

The final results of global monitoring activities are regulatory, enforcement and personnel changes at the federal and regional levels.

2.5. Utilisation of local monitoring results

Following the judge's consideration of an individual case, the further actions of the defence counsel and the defendant depend on the judge's conduct during the trial. If the judge has deliberately committed violations indicating that he or she has committed a disciplinary offence or an offence, his or her further unlawful activities should be prevented by filing a number of special complaints and

---

[23] Shulipa Yu. 10 reasons of illegal collusion of traffic police and courts. M-2011. Moscow branch of FAR: http://www.far-msk.ru/?p=13090

applications.

In order not to expose the defendant and defence counsel to the judge, it is advisable to entrust representatives of the public to appeal against unlawful actions of the presiding officer.

Having analysed with the public the identified violations of the judge, it is necessary to immediately draw up and send collective complaints to the bodies of the judicial community and to the chairpersons (district, city) and regional courts competent to make a submission to the Qualification Collegium of Judges on bringing the judge to disciplinary responsibility. In addition, a collective complaint should be filed with the Chairperson of the relevant Qualification Collegium of Judges.

As a rule, the defence counsel can provide a more objective legal assessment of the judge's actions than the members of the public present in the room. Therefore, the defence counsel can take care of drafting complaints and sending them out, and members of the public will only have to sign the complaints. The complaint must be accompanied by a transcript of the court session with an electronic medium of audio and/or video recording. In the annex to the transcript it is necessary to indicate the make and model of the technical means of audio and (or) video recording, the place and time of its implementation and authenticate the submitted material with the signatures of the persons indicated in the complaint.

Remind the presidents of (district, city) and regional courts that the right to publicise the audio and/or video recording made remains.

Referring to part 1 of Article 21 No. 30-FZ of 14 March 2002. "On Bodies of the Judicial Community in the Russian Federation" and para. 3 of Article 28 of the Regulation on the Procedure of the Qualification Collegiums of Judges (approved by the All-Russian Commission of the Qualification Collegiums of Judges on 22 March 2007), it should be recalled that the applicants were invited as interested parties to the disciplinary proceedings against the judge. It should also be mentioned that the defendant and defence counsel should be summoned to the disciplinary proceedings, but as witnesses to the commission of a disciplinary offence.

If this complaint receives an unmotivated response from the above-mentioned judicial officials, it is necessary to appeal against their actions in not taking appropriate response measures in an extrajudicial (administrative) order to the chairmen of the Supreme Court of the Russian Federation and the Supreme Court of the Russian Federation and further continue to complain up to the President of the Russian Federation.

A miscarriage of justice, being always an offence, is a complex legal composition, the elements of which are:

1. *unlawful behaviour of the court;*
2. *the presence of harmful effects;*
3. *causal link between the unlawful behaviour of the court and the resulting harmful consequences.*

In individual cases, there may be a fourth element - the fault of the court (intentional or negligent).

The unlawful behaviour of the court is its volitional action (or inaction), which does not comply with legal prescriptions, infringes the subjective rights of the participants of the process, does not agree with the legal obligations imposed on the court.[24]

Let us consider the four main ways of bringing a judge and a traffic police inspector to criminal responsibility.

---

[24] Law Enforcement: Theory and Practice. Formula of Law M-2008 p 326. Editor-in-Chief Tikhomirov Yu.

1) <u>Submitting a criminal complaint to the Chairman of the Investigative Committee of the Russian Federation.</u>

If during the court proceedings and (or) after them in the actions of the judge and (or) traffic police inspector there are signs of a crime, it is necessary to immediately report the crime committed.

It is possible, directly in the course of the trial, unnoticed by the judge on tel. 911, inform the police of the fact of the committed (in progress) offence and request a visit to the scene of the incident by the SOG directly to the court. Such actions are not prohibited by law. All incoming calls to police units are recorded and logged in accordance with the established procedure. After the arrival of the SOG, it is necessary to demand from the police officers to draw up a report of the inspection of the scene of the incident (Articles 176 - 177 of the Criminal Procedure Code of the Russian Federation). And in the presence of members of the public.

Such action will facilitate the more rapid initiation of criminal proceedings against the judge.

According to para. 5 part. 1 of Article 448 of the Code of Criminal Procedure of the Russian Federation, the decision to initiate criminal proceedings against a justice of the peace (federal) is taken by the Chairman of the Investigative Committee of the Russian Federation with the consent of the relevant qualification collegium of judges.

In accordance with paras. B para. 1 part. 2 of Article 151 of the Criminal Procedure Code of the Russian Federation preliminary investigation is carried out by investigators in criminal cases on offences committed by officials of internal affairs bodies.

It is worth considering that it is much more difficult to initiate criminal proceedings against a serving traffic police inspector or judge than disciplinary proceedings.

The practice of filing applications to investigative departments and offices of the Investigative Committee of the Russian Federation in accordance with article 141 of the Code of Criminal Procedure about crimes committed by officials and judges shows that investigators of these bodies practically do not register citizens' applications about crimes, do not issue notification coupons to citizens, do not consider applications about crimes in accordance with the procedure established by law and do not issue rulings on them based on the law, which makes it possible to hide criminals acting in their official capacity from justice.[25]

After the entry into force of p. 2.4 of the Instruction on the procedure for consideration of appeals and reception of citizens in the prosecutor's office (approved by Order of the Prosecutor General of the Russian Federation No. 212 of 27.12.2007), *and* subparagraph 2 of para. 21 of the Instruction on the procedure for receipt, registration and verification of crime reports in the investigative bodies (investigative units) of the system of the Investigative Committee of the Russian Federation (approved by Order of the Chairman of the Investigative Committee of the Russian Federation No. 72 of 3 May 2011), the illegal practice of concealing a certain category of officials and judges from criminal prosecution has taken root.

Often, when refusing to consider applications about crimes committed by subjects of special criminal prosecution, investigators of the Investigative Committee refer to paragraph 2 of clause 21, according to which applications in which applicants express their disagreement with the decisions of officials taken by them within the limits of the powers provided for by law and in this connection raise the question of bringing them to justice, suggesting the possible commission of an official offence, do not require verification in accordance with the procedure provided for in articles 144 and 145 of the Criminal Procedure Code of the Russian Federation. 144, 145 OF THE CODE OF

---

[25] Shulipa Y. Y. Moscow judge legalised official offences. M-2011. Moscow branch of FAR: http://www.far-msk.ru/?p=9615

CRIMINAL PROCEDURE OF THE RUSSIAN FEDERATION.

By the decision of the Supreme Court of the Russian Federation of 13 January 2010 No. GKPI09-1542, the previously valid paragraph 4 of point 33 of the Instruction, approved by Order of the First Deputy Prosecutor General of the Russian Federation - Chairman of the Investigative Committee of the Russian Federation of 7 September 2007 No. 14, and point 2.4. Instruction on the procedure of consideration of appeals and reception of citizens in the prosecutor's office, approved by Order of the Prosecutor General of the Russian Federation of 26 December 2006 No. 120, the legality of which was previously confirmed by the decision of the Supreme Court of the Russian Federation of 26 November 2007 No. GKPI07-1142, are not considered to be contrary to federal law or other normative legal act having greater legal force.

Meanwhile, the judgement in question establishes that the contested legal norm <u>does not exclude the obligation of officials, within the limits of their competence, to verify such applications and take decisions on them in accordance with the</u> procedure provided for in Articles 144 and 145 of the Code of Criminal Procedure.

This provision of the decision of the Supreme Court of the Russian Federation from 13. 01. 2010 № GKPI09-1542 should be referred to in complaints when appealing against illegal actions of investigators of investigative departments and departments of the Investigative Committee of the Russian Federation.

In spite of this, there is a widespread investigative practice where investigators of investigative departments and directorates of the Investigative Committee of the Investigative Committee of the Russian Federation refer to statements submitted by applicants about criminal offences committed by judges and officials as appeals or petitions.

In the case of receipt on the application filed in accordance with Art. 141 of the CPC of the RF, instead of the decision established by law (Art. 5, Art. 145 of the CPC of the RF), instead of a response-answer or a decision to refuse to satisfy the application, it is necessary to appeal against the actions of the investigator on the investigative or prosecutor's line. The complaint in accordance with Article 124 of the RF CCrimP of Criminal Procedure must be considered by the prosecutor, head of the investigative body within 3 days from the day of its receipt. In exceptional cases, when in order to verify the complaint it is necessary to request additional materials or take other measures, it is allowed to consider the complaint within 10 days, of which the applicant is notified. However, in practice, these time limits for consideration of complaints are almost never observed.

Thus, when appealing against unlawful actions of an investigator in the prosecutor-investigator line, it is possible to reach the Prosecutor General of the Russian Federation within a month, and then complain to the Prosecutor General - to the President of the Russian Federation.

Given the current law enforcement practice, appealing to the court in accordance with Article 125 of the Criminal Procedural Code of the RF is not only useless, but also carries a real threat.[26] If the judge leaves the filed complaint without satisfaction, and the judicial board of the regional court leaves it in force, the effective ruling will confirm the legality and validity of the actions of the investigator. The enforceable court ruling will cover the investigator as a protective letter against further appeal against his actions.

In parallel, while the stages of appealing the actions of the investigator are taking place, the defence counsel (defendant) to ensure the criminal prosecution of a corrupt judge and (or) traffic police inspector should use the rest of the legal tools in full.

---

[26] Op. cit.

2) <u>Filing a report on an offence committed outside the jurisdiction of investigation</u>.

According to the Instruction on the Unified Crime Record (approved by Orders of the Prosecutor General's Office of the Russian Federation, the Ministry of Internal Affairs, the Ministry of Emergency Situations, the Ministry of Justice, the Federal Security Service, the Ministry of Economic Development and the Federal Drug Control Service of 29 December 2005 No. 39 / No. 1070 / No. 1021 / No. 253 / No. 780 / No. 353 / No. 399, (D)), a statement about a crime committed, including by a judge, may be filed with any of the above-mentioned agencies.

Officials of these agencies, in accordance with paragraph 3, part 1, article 145 of the Code of Criminal Procedure. Article 145(1)(3) of the Code of Criminal Procedure of the Russian Federation requires them to issue a decision to refer the report for investigation in accordance with Article 151 of this Code. As a rule, the above-mentioned agencies do not have any problems with the registration of statements about offences committed.

Based on the provision of part 1 of article 141 of the Code of Criminal Procedure of the Russian Federation, the decision to refer the application for investigation must be issued within no more than 3 days from the date of receipt of the said communication.

Since the statement about the committed crime was submitted to the investigator directly not from a particular citizen, but sent on the basis of the decision of the official authorised by the norms of the CPC to carry out criminal prosecution, registered and entered in the state statistics of the investigator of the Investigative Committee of the Russian Federation, the investigator is obliged to consider the statement received by him and to take a procedural decision based on the law in accordance with paragraphs 1 and 2 of part 1 of part 1 of article 145 of the CPC of the Russian Federation. 1 of Article 145(1) of the Code of Criminal Procedure of the Russian Federation.

3) <u>Initiating a criminal case with the help of the media and the internet</u>.

Information received from other sources, such as the media, may be the reason for initiating criminal proceedings (Clause 3 of Article 140 of the RF CCP).

The video recording made during the court hearing or directly during the dialogue with the traffic police inspector should be immediately uploaded to one of the major Internet portals, e.g. Youtube. When posting the video, it is necessary to describe in detail the name and address of the court, the initials of the presiding judge and the persons involved in the case.

Briefly describe the essence of the case and the essence of the offence or crime committed by the judge and (or) traffic police inspector. After that, via e-mail to pass the information to the relevant public associations.

Public representatives invited to court hearings are themselves members of various public associations. As is well known, public associations co-operate with the media in their respective fields, which enables them to assist in the prompt reporting of information.

According to Article 2 of the Law of the Russian Federation of 27. 12. 1991 N 2124-1 "On Mass Media", a mass media outlet is understood to be a periodical printed publication, radio, television, video programme, newsreel programme, other form of periodical dissemination of mass information. Within the meaning of this legal provision, another form of mass information dissemination is the Internet.

In accordance with part 2 of article 144 of the Code of Criminal Procedure of the Russian Federation, an enquiry body, on the instructions of the procurator, and also on the instructions of the head of the investigative body, an investigator shall conduct a check on a report of an offence disseminated in the media.

After the publication, announcement or display in the media and the Internet of information indicating the commission of an offence by a traffic police inspector and (or) judge, it is necessary to send an application for an investigation on this fact, as previously stated, to a body not under investigation.

Practice shows that after this information is covered in the federal and even regional mass media, the actions of traffic police inspectors begin to be checked on the initiative of the relevant units of the RSD.[27]

4) <u>Publicising the facts of an offence committed at a community event</u>.

As is known, according to Article 31 of the Constitution of the Russian Federation, citizens have the right to assemble peacefully without arms, to hold meetings, rallies and demonstrations, marches and picketing.

If the authorities do not take action against offenders acting in an official capacity, it is possible to force them to take action through public events.

Mass public events attract some regional and federal media. Thus, it is also possible to cover the evidence of the committed offences through the media representatives present at the rally. In the light of the Resolution of the Constitutional Court of the Russian Federation of 18.10.2011 N 23-P, a judge cannot be held criminally liable for passing a knowingly unjust verdict or other judicial act if this oppression has entered into legal force and has not been cancelled in accordance with the procedure established by the procedural legislation. An unlawful act that has entered into legal force becomes at the same time a defence of the judge against criminal prosecution. In other cases, it is possible to initiate criminal prosecution of a judge for knowingly making false information in documents (Art. 292 of the Criminal Code of the Russian Federation).

In other words, only a well-coordinated interaction between the defence counsel, the defendant, representatives of a public association, the media and a number of specialists can not only cross the existing vicious law enforcement practice, but also rehabilitate persons previously illegally brought to administrative responsibility.

Conclusion

These problems lead to the conclusion that at the current stage of state and legal development of Russia it is impossible to eliminate corruption and various abuses by traffic police inspectors and judges of courts of general jurisdiction on the initiative of competent officials of public authorities. For the time being, public associations and individual initiative citizens can move officials to radical systemic changes, thanks to the results obtained through public control activities.

Now it is impossible to solve these problems "from above". Therefore, the citizens of Russia need to solve the problems "from below" independently through strict self-organisation using any means not prohibited by law.

The use of the results of judicial monitoring can change not only the vicious judicial law enforcement practice, but also eliminate the biased, irresponsible and formal attitude of the traffic <u>police</u> leadership to the organisation and conduct of work on the prevention of DTA, the desire for only formal and quantitative indicators of activity related to raids, special operations, preventive measures, detection of "offences".

<u>Court monitoring has made it possible to identify quickly</u>:

1) corruption crossroads;

2) Acts of officials that are not based on the law (protocols, rulings and *other documents of traffic police inspectors):*

3) judicial acts not based on law;

---

[27] Op. cit.

4)   Committing administrative and disciplinary offences, as well as criminal offences, by traffic police inspectors and judges of courts of general jurisdiction;

5)   various abuses by presidents of courts of general jurisdiction;

6)   the judge's dependence on traffic police inspectors for baselessly issuing guilty verdicts; and further use the results obtained in the manner prescribed by law.

If properly organised, judicial monitoring will become an indispensable public tool to encourage officials and judges to carry out their professional duties within the law.

The development of judicial monitoring and its results should contribute to the change of federal legislation in the administrative and jurisdictional sphere of traffic police units and courts of general jurisdiction, as well as in the field of road safety.

All of this opens up great prospects for judicial monitoring.

The results of the judicial monitoring revealed the main vices of the Russian justice system and the traffic police, which can be divided into two parts.

One part of the above-mentioned vices of the traffic police and courts lies in significant shortcomings of the current legislation of the Russian Federation, - the other part lies in improper and biased state administration.

Therefore, at this stage of the state-legal development of the country, in our opinion, it is necessary to substantially renew the senior staff of the courts and the traffic police and at the same time to implement the following legislative and regulatory changes.

1. *It is necessary to cancel the provisions of the order of the Ministry of Internal Affairs of the Russian Federation No. 25 of 19.01.2010 "On the issues of evaluation of the performance of internal affairs bodies of the Russian Federation". "On Issues of Evaluation of the Activity of Internal Affairs Bodies of the Russian Federation" in terms of retaining the rules according to which IAB units cannot reduce the number of prosecuted persons as compared to the same period of the previous year if they want to receive a positive evaluation of their activity.*

2. *Change the criteria for judges' performance by prohibiting the evaluation of their performance by the volume of cases they have heard.*

3. *Increase the positive performance of judges depending on the decrease in the number of complaints against judicial acts adopted by them or their actions (in other words, fewer complaints, higher positive result).*

4. *In accordance with Article 10 of the Constitution of the Russian Federation, to prohibit joint meetings of justices of the peace and federal judges with representatives of the traffic police on issues of joint law enforcement.*

5. *Prohibit traffic police inspectors from personally submitting cases on administrative offences to judges for consideration.*

6. *To recognise the CAO RF as null and void.*

7. *To enact new legislation on administrative offences:*

o *Administrative Code.*

o *Code of Administrative Procedure.*

o *Administrative and Enforcement Code.*

8. *To introduce into the Administrative Code a norm providing for administrative responsibility for unlawful bringing of a citizen to administrative responsibility (by analogy with article 299 of the Criminal Code of the Russian Federation).*

9. *Significantly strengthen normative control by the courts, the management of traffic police departments and prosecutors' offices over the jurisdictional activities of traffic police inspectors in drawing up procedural documents, initiating cases of administrative offences*

and issuing rulings.

10. *Significantly strengthen judicial norm control on the part of the Presidium of the Supreme Court of the Russian Federation and presidiums of regional courts for judicial acts of magistrate and federal judges in cases of administrative offences by adopting a relevant resolution of the plenum.*

11. *Introduce a provision in the Code of Administrative Procedure that allows for both judicial and extrajudicial appeal against any action of a traffic police inspector (by analogy with Articles 123 - 125 of the CPC of the Russian Federation).*

12. *In the Federal Law "On Police", as well as in the relevant codes, establish the types of responsibility of police officers for committing certain offences and crimes.*

13. *Introduce a provision in the Code of Administrative Procedure requiring judges, bodies and officials, at the request of participants in a case, to ensure that court hearings are video-recorded.*

14. *Modernise legislation in the field of standardisation, metrology and telemetry by introducing norms establishing quality standards for measuring instruments.*

15. *For drivers driving vehicles under the influence of alcohol or drugs, federal law should establish differentiated administrative liability depending on the degree of intoxication.*

16. *To equip the medical rooms of drug addiction doctors where examinations are carried out with video and sound recording devices.*

17. *To establish a special norm in the Administrative Code, authorising bringing narcologists for violation of technologies (methods) of medical examination to stricter administrative responsibility than experts and specialists. For falsification of the results of medical examinations, drug addiction doctors should be brought to administrative responsibility by disqualifying them for up to three years.*

18. *To introduce and legislate a more perfect method of determining alcohol or drug intoxication in the organism of a person driving a vehicle not only by the presence of a certain amount of absolute ethyl alcohol in the organism, but also by taking into account the totality of a number of clinical signs of intoxication, based on the general clinical picture of the physical condition of the witness.*

19. *To recognise the RF PDD as null and void.*

20. *To put into effect a single codified act regulating legal relations in the field of road safety "Road Code" of the Russian Federation by "audifying some norms of the Federal Law "On Road Safety", the current traffic rules of the Russian Federation, the Federal Law "On CMTPL insurance of vehicle owners", GOSTR 52289 - 2004.*

Bibliography

1) Shulipa Y. Y. Moscow judge legalised official offences. M-2010. Moscow branch of FAR: www.far-msk.ru/?p=9615

2) Shulipa Yu. Yu. How to a driver to appeal against a resolution on a case about an administrative offence? M - 2008. Electrotransport.ru: electrotransport.ru/ussr/ index.php/ topic,397.0.html

3) Ibid.

4) Ibid.

5) Shulipa Yu. Yu. Diagnostics of Moscow administrative justice. First results on the example of corruption crossroads - Paveletskaya Square of Moscow. Moscow. Scientific and practical report. M-2011. Moscow branch of FAR: www.far- msk.ru/?page_id=11241

6) Ibid.

7) Decision of the Deputy Chairman of the Moscow City Court of 17. 12. 2010, № 4a-3528/10

8) Commission reveals joint traffic police and judicial methods of deceiving citizens. M - 2011. Moscow branch of FAR: wwwfar-msk.ru/?p=12164

9) Shulipa Y. Y. Comments on law enforcement practice. M- 2008. Era-auto: www.car-era.ru/articles/2685.html

10) Information letter of the Arkhangelsk Regional Court of 27.12.2005 on the consideration of cases on administrative offences in the field of road traffic.

11) Shulipa Yu. Arbitrariness of traffic police and courts. Materials of press conference on 1 December 2010. Moscow branch of FAR: www.far-msk.ru/?p=10594

12) Ibid.

13) Shulipa Yu. Yu. How to ruin a fabricated case and stay with the rights? M. - 2011. Moscow branch of FAR: http://wwwfar-msk.ru/?p=16155

14) Shulipa Yu. Winter exposure of OPT narcologists, IDPS and judges. M - 2011. Moscow branch of FAR: http://www.far-msk.ru/?p=17395

15) Road traps have been placed on the Moscow map. ITAR-TASS /Interpress/M. 2011: http://www.firstnews.ru/news/lenta/20056/

16) C. I. Ozhegov, Dictionary of the Russian Language. Onyx and Education. M - 2007.

17) Shulipa Y. Yu. Technology of counteraction to unlawful collusion of traffic police and courts. M. - 2011. Moscow branch of FAR: http://www.far-msk.ru/?p=13563

18) NTV story about the "trap" at Paveletskiy railway station from 03 July 2010: http://www.youtube.com/watch?v=LD94X0zTyz8

19) Voyevodin V. A. Paveletskaya - continuation of history. M-2010. Moscow branch of FAR: http://www.far-msk.ru/?p=7849

20) Shulipa Y. Y. 10 reasons of illegal collusion of traffic police *and* courts. M-2011. Moscow branch of FAR: http://www.far-msk.ru/?p=13090

Statutory Instruments.
(as of 01 February 2012)

1) Convention for the Protection of Human Rights and Fundamental Freedoms (Rome, 4 November 1950);

2) Constitution of the Russian Federation (adopted by popular vote on 12 December 2012);

3) Criminal Code of the Russian Federation of 13.06.1996 N 63-FZ;

4) Criminal Procedure Code of the Russian Federation of 18.12.2001 N 174-FZ;

5) Code of the Russian Federation on Administrative Offences of 30 December 2001 N 195-FZ;

6) Federal Law "On the Prosecutor's Office of the Russian Federation" of 17. 01. 1992 N 2202-I;

7) Federal Law "On the procedure for consideration of appeals of citizens of the Russian Federation" of 02.05.2006 N 59-FZ;

8) Federal Law "On Bodies of the Judicial Community" of 14 March 2002, N 30-FZ;

9) Federal Law "On Public Associations" of 19.05.1995 N 82-FZ;

11) Federal Law "On Police" of 07. 02. 2011 N 3-FZ;

12) Federal Law "On Ensuring Access to Information on the Activities of Courts in the Russian Federation" dated 22 December 2008 N 262-FZ;

13) Federal Law "On Information, Information Technologies and Information Protection" dated 27 July 2006 No. 149-FZ;

14) Law of the Russian Federation "On the Status of Judges in the Russian Federation" of 26.06.1992 N 3132-1;

15) Law of the Russian Federation "On Mass Media" of 27. 12. 1991 N 2124-1.

16) Administrative Regulations of the Ministry of Internal Affairs of the Russian Federation of the execution of the state function to control and supervise the compliance of road users with the requirements in the field of road safety (approved by Order of the Ministry of Internal Affairs of the Russian Federation № 185 of 02. 03. 2009);

17) Instruction on the organisation of activities of the road patrol service of the State Inspectorate for Road Traffic Safety of the Ministry of Internal Affairs of the Russian Federation (approved by Order of the Ministry of Internal Affairs of the Russian Federation No. 186 of 02.03.2009 DSP);

18) Instruction on the procedure for receiving, registering and resolving in the internal affairs bodies of the Russian Federation statements, reports and other information about incidents (approved by Order of the Ministry of Internal Affairs of the Russian Federation of 4 May 2010 N 333);

19) Instruction on the Unified Crime Record (approved by orders of the Prosecutor General's Office of the Russian Federation, the Ministry of Internal Affairs, the Ministry of Emergency Situations, the Ministry of Justice, the Federal Security Service, the Ministry of Economic Development and the Federal Drug Control Service of 29 December 2005, No. 39 / No. 1070 / No. 1021 / No. 253 / No. 780 / No. 353 / No. 399, (D));

20) Instruction on the procedure for consideration of appeals and reception of citizens in the prosecutor's office (approved by Order of the Prosecutor General of the Russian Federation No. 212 of 27.12.2007);

21) Instruction on the order of receipt, registration and verification of crime reports in investigative bodies (investigative units) of the system of the Investigative Committee of the Russian Federation (approved by Order of the Chairman of the Investigative Committee of the Russian Federation dated 3 May 2011 No. 72);
(approved by Order No. 14 of the Chairman of the Investigative Committee of the Russian Federation dated 07.09.2007);

22) Regulations on the Procedure for the Work of Qualification Collegiums of Judges (approved by the All-Russian Commission of Qualification Collegiums of Judges on 22 March 2007).

For notes

Printed by Books on Demand GmbH, Norderstedt / Germany